HELLO

This Log Book is designed to help you take care of your garden. The information it contains will enable you to:

- ★ plan your year-round goals,
- ★ design a planting scheme,
- ★ decide which plants to plant each month,
- ★ control plant diseases, etc.

This year you will enjoy a beautiful allotment garden and the opportunity to relax in it

If you enjoyed this log book, please leave us a review. Your opinion is very important to us. We will be very grateful

My Goals & Plans Calendar

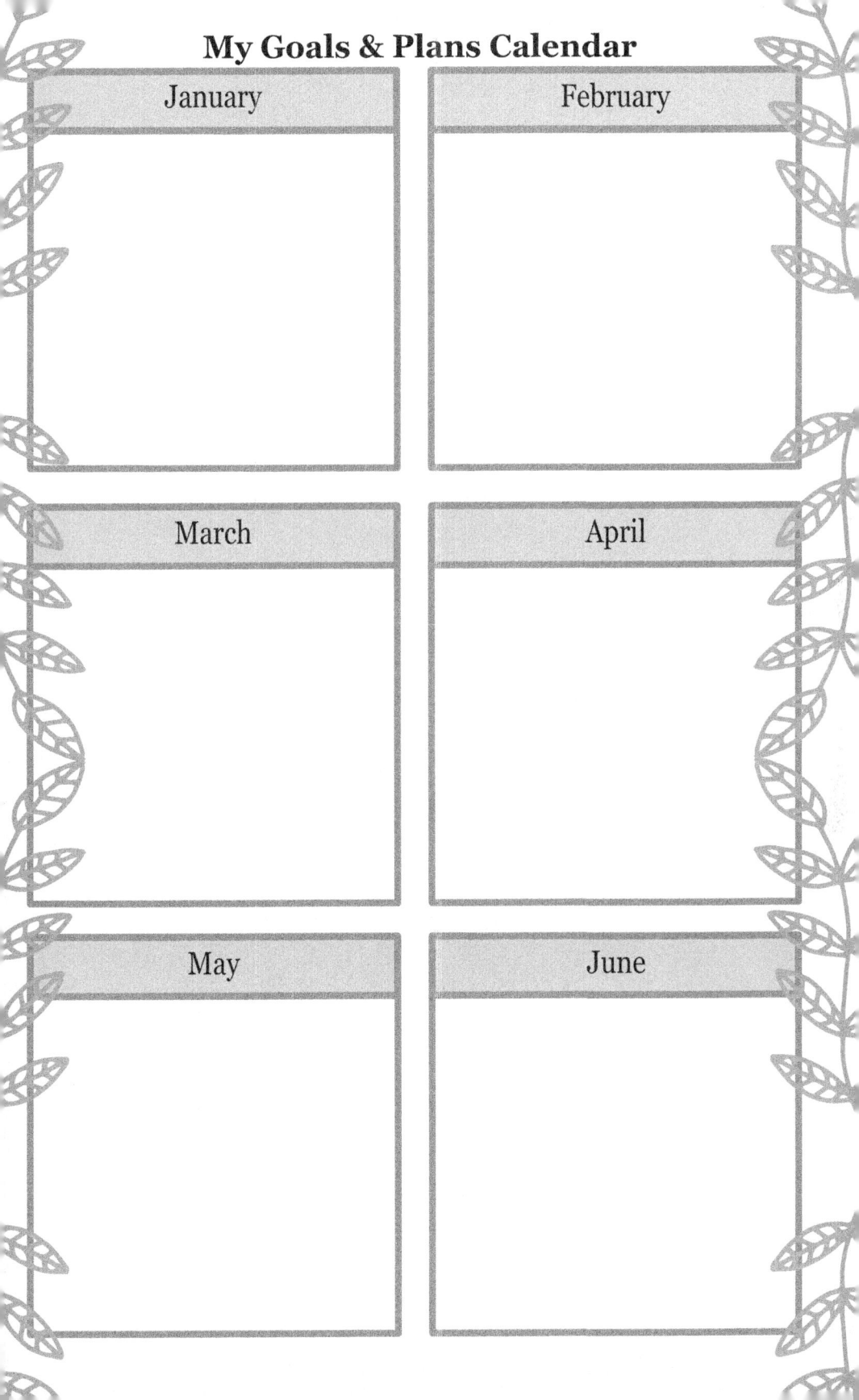

January

February

March

April

May

June

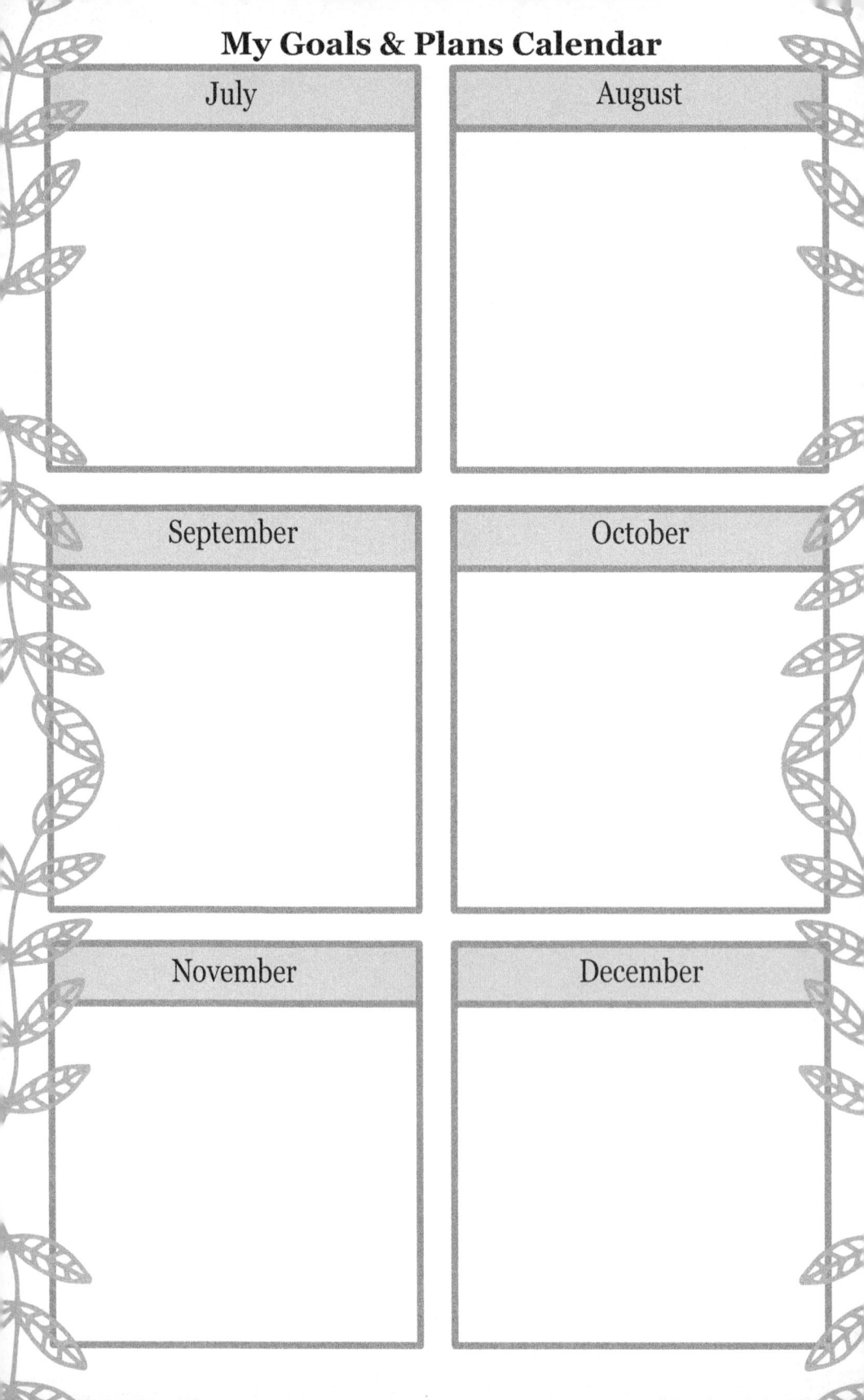

Garden Map

Monthly Planting Planner

Plant Name	January	February	March	April	May	June	July	August	September	October	November	December

* You can mark each month with a different colour to make the table clearer.

Monthly Planting Planner

Plant Name	January	February	March	April	May	June	July	August	September	October	November	December

* You can mark each month with a different colour to make the table clearer.

Monthly Harvest Calendar

January

February

March

April

May

June

July

August

September

October

November

December

My Weekly Plans

Task	Date	M	T	W	Th	F	S	Su

My Weekly Plans

Task	Date	M	T	W	Th	F	S	Su

My Weekly Plans

Task	Date	M	T	W	Th	F	S	Su

My Spend

Date	Fruits	Vegis	Herbs	Shrubs	Flowers	Trees	Grass	Equipment	Other	TOTAL
TOTAL										

My Spend

Date	Fruits	Vegis	Herbs	Shrubs	Flowers	Trees	Grass	Equipment	Other	TOTAL
TOTAL										

Seedlings Log

Variety	Indoor Start	Transplant On	Row	Harvested On

Seedlings Log

Variety	Indoor Start	Transplant On	Row	Harvested On

Plants Log

Plants	Qty	Row	Planted On	Harvested On

Plants Log

Plants	Qty	Row	Planted On	Harvested On

Plants Log

Plants	Qty	Row	Planted On	Harvested On

Seeds Packet Info

Crop/Variety	Sowing Depth	Days to Geminate	Days to Maturity	Harvested Window

Seeds Packet Info

Crop/Variety	Sowing Depth	Days to Geminate	Days to Maturity	Harvested Window

Pest Control

Bed/Row	Crop/Family	Pest	Disease	Treatment

Pest Control

Bed/Row	Crop/Family	Pest	Disease	Treatment

Pest Control

Bed/Row	Crop/Family	Pest	Disease	Treatment

Notes

Plant Name _____

Purchased At _____ Price _____

Date Planted _____ Harvested _____

Planted from   Seeds ☐   Transplant ☐

Plant Type

Fruit ❀	Vegetable ❀	Flower ❀
Herb ❀	Shrub ❀	Tree ❀
Seedling ❀	Annual ❀	Biennial ❀
Perennial ❀	Grass ❀	Weed ❀

Water Requirement   A little 💧   AVG 💧💧   A Lot 💧💧💧

Sunlight Needed   A little ☀   AVG ☀☀   A Lot ☀☀☀

Fertilizers Used

Rating   ## Notes

Size   ☆ ☆ ☆ ☆ ☆

Color   ☆ ☆ ☆ ☆ ☆

Taste   ☆ ☆ ☆ ☆ ☆

What's Working? | What's not Working?

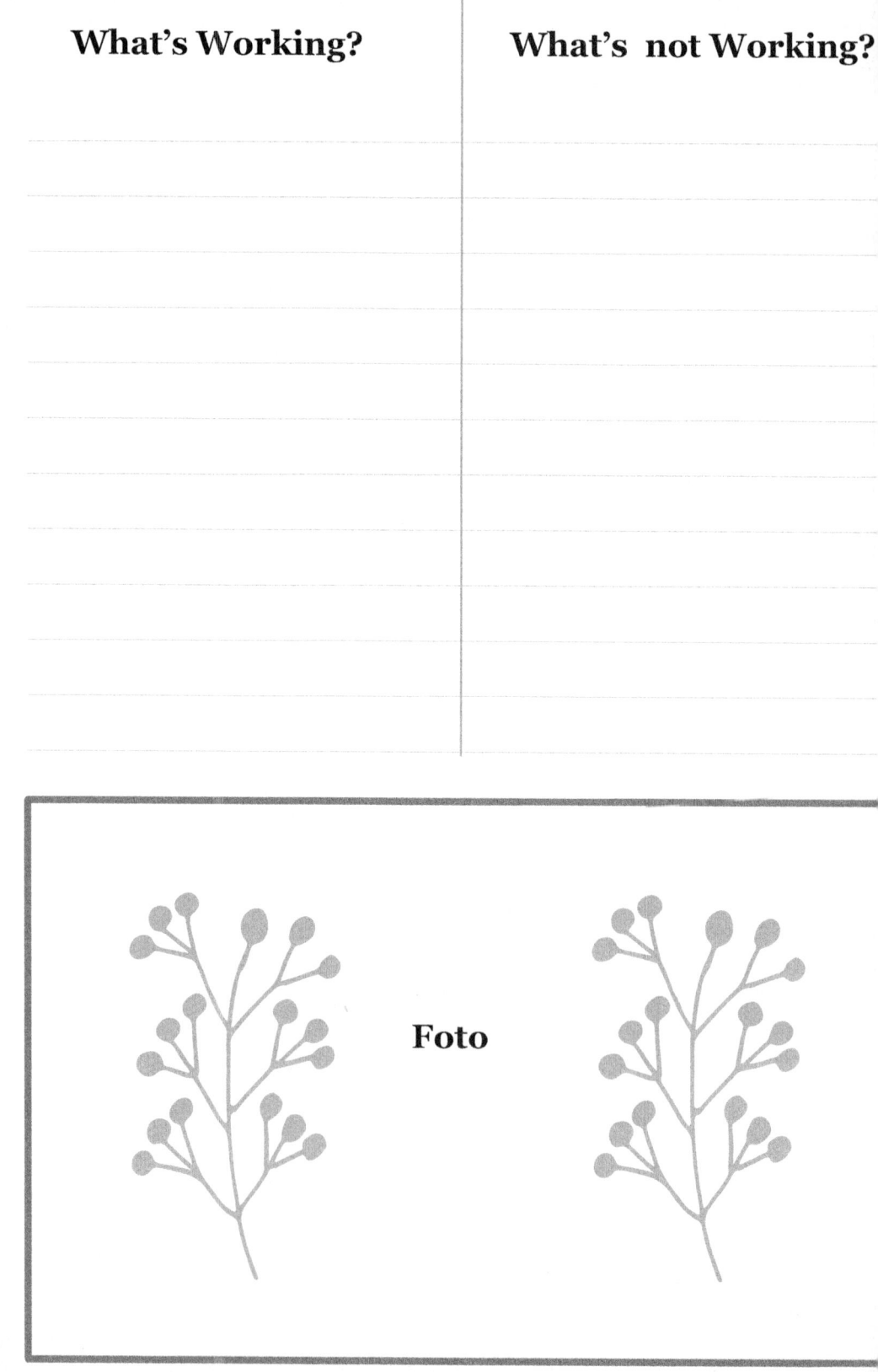

Foto

Plant Name: _____

Purchased At: _____ Price: _____

Date Planted: _____ Harvested: _____

Planted from   Seeds ☐   Transplant ☐

Plant Type

Fruit ○	Vegetable ○	Flower ○
Herb ○	Shrub ○	Tree ○
Seedling ○	Annual ○	Biennial ○
Perennial ○	Grass ○	Weed ○

Water Requirement   A little 💧   AVG 💧💧   A Lot 💧💧💧

Sunlight Needed   A little ☼   AVG ☼☼   A Lot ☼☼☼

Fertilizers Used _____

Rating

Size   ☆ ☆ ☆ ☆ ☆
Color ☆ ☆ ☆ ☆ ☆
Taste ☆ ☆ ☆ ☆ ☆

Notes

What's Working?	**What's not Working?**

Foto

Plant Name _____

Purchased At _____   Price _____

Date Planted _____   Harvested _____

Planted from   Seeds ☐   Transplant ☐

Plant Type

Fruit	Vegetable	Flower
Herb	Shrub	Tree
Seedling	Annual	Biennial
Perennial	Grass	Weed

Water Requirement   A little   AVG   A Lot

Sunlight Needed   A little   AVG   A Lot

Fertilizers Used _____

Rating

Size   ☆ ☆ ☆ ☆ ☆

Color   ☆ ☆ ☆ ☆ ☆

Taste   ☆ ☆ ☆ ☆ ☆

Notes

What's Working?	What's not Working?

Plant Name _____

Purchased At _____   Price _____

Date Planted _____   Harvested _____

Planted from   Seeds ☐   Transplant ☐

Plant Type

Fruit ◯	Vegetable ◯	Flower ◯
Herb ◯	Shrub ◯	Tree ◯
Seedling ◯	Annual ◯	Biennial ◯
Perennial ◯	Grass ◯	Weed ◯

Water Requirement   A little 💧   AVG 💧💧   A Lot 💧💧💧

Sunlight Needed   A little ☀   AVG ☀☀   A Lot ☀☀☀

Fertilizers Used _____

Rating   ## Notes

Size   ☆ ☆ ☆ ☆ ☆

Color   ☆ ☆ ☆ ☆ ☆

Taste   ☆ ☆ ☆ ☆ ☆

What's Working?

What's not Working?

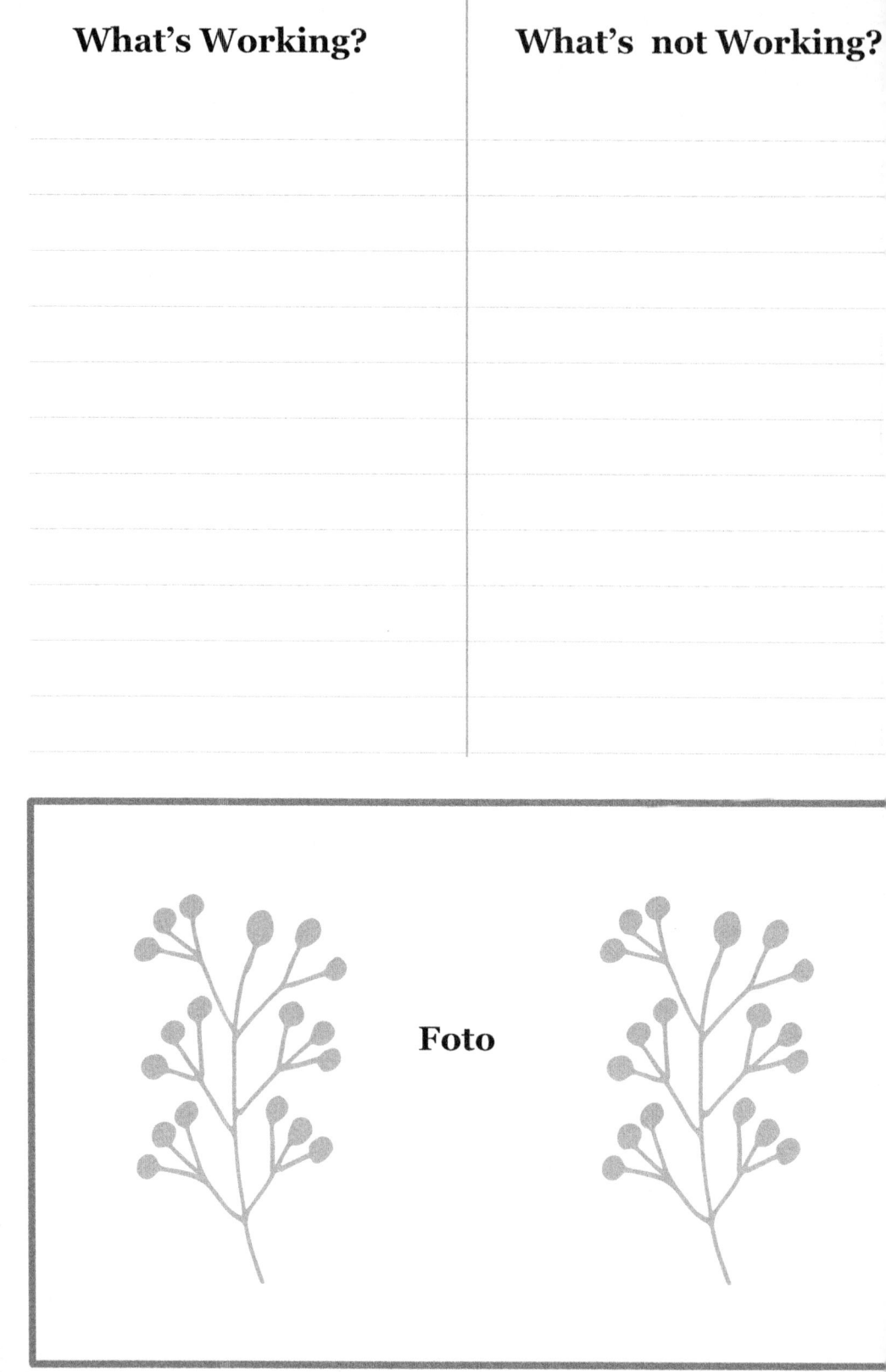

Foto

Plant Name _____

Purchased At _____   Price _____

Date Planted _____   Harvested _____

Planted from   Seeds ☐   Transplant ☐

Plant Type

Fruit ○	Vegetable ○	Flower ○
Herb ○	Shrub ○	Tree ○
Seedling ○	Annual ○	Biennial ○
Perennial ○	Grass ○	Weed ○

Water Requirement   A little 💧   AVG 💧💧   A Lot 💧💧💧

Sunlight Needed   A little ☀   AVG ☀☀   A Lot ☀☀☀

Fertilizers Used _____

Rating   ## Notes

Size   ☆ ☆ ☆ ☆ ☆
Color   ☆ ☆ ☆ ☆ ☆
Taste   ☆ ☆ ☆ ☆ ☆

What's Working? | What's not Working?

Foto

Plant Name _____

Purchased At _____ Price _____

Date Planted _____ Harvested _____

Planted from   Seeds ☐   Transplant ☐

Plant Type

Fruit ✿	Vegetable ✿	Flower ✿
Herb ✿	Shrub ✿	Tree ✿
Seedling ✿	Annual ✿	Biennial ✿
Perennial ✿	Grass ✿	Weed ✿

Water Requirement   A little 💧   AVG 💧💧   A Lot 💧💧💧

Sunlight Needed   A little ☀   AVG ☀☀   A Lot ☀☀☀

Fertilizers Used _____

Rating   Notes

Size   ☆ ☆ ☆ ☆ ☆

Color   ☆ ☆ ☆ ☆ ☆

Taste   ☆ ☆ ☆ ☆ ☆

What's Working?	What's not Working?

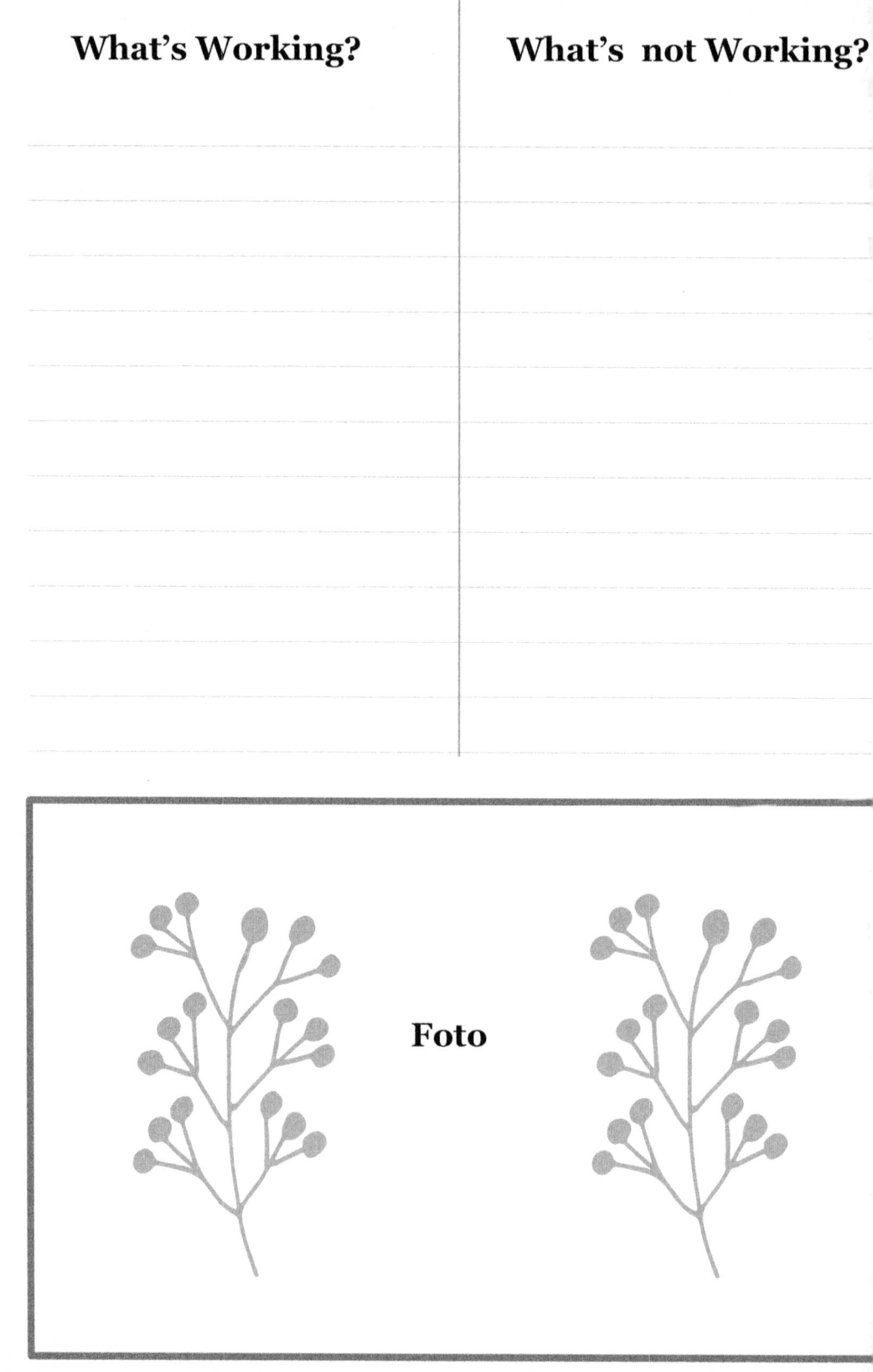

Plant Name _____

Purchased At _____ Price _____

Date Planted _____ Harvested _____

Planted from   Seeds ☐   Transplant ☐

Plant Type

Fruit ○	Vegetable ○	Flower ○
Herb ○	Shrub ○	Tree ○
Seedling ○	Annual ○	Biennial ○
Perennial ○	Grass ○	Weed ○

Water Requirement   A little 💧   AVG 💧💧   A Lot 💧💧💧

Sunlight Needed   A little ☀   AVG ☀☀   A Lot ☀☀☀

Fertilizers Used _____

Rating   ## Notes

Size   ☆ ☆ ☆ ☆ ☆
Color ☆ ☆ ☆ ☆ ☆
Taste ☆ ☆ ☆ ☆ ☆

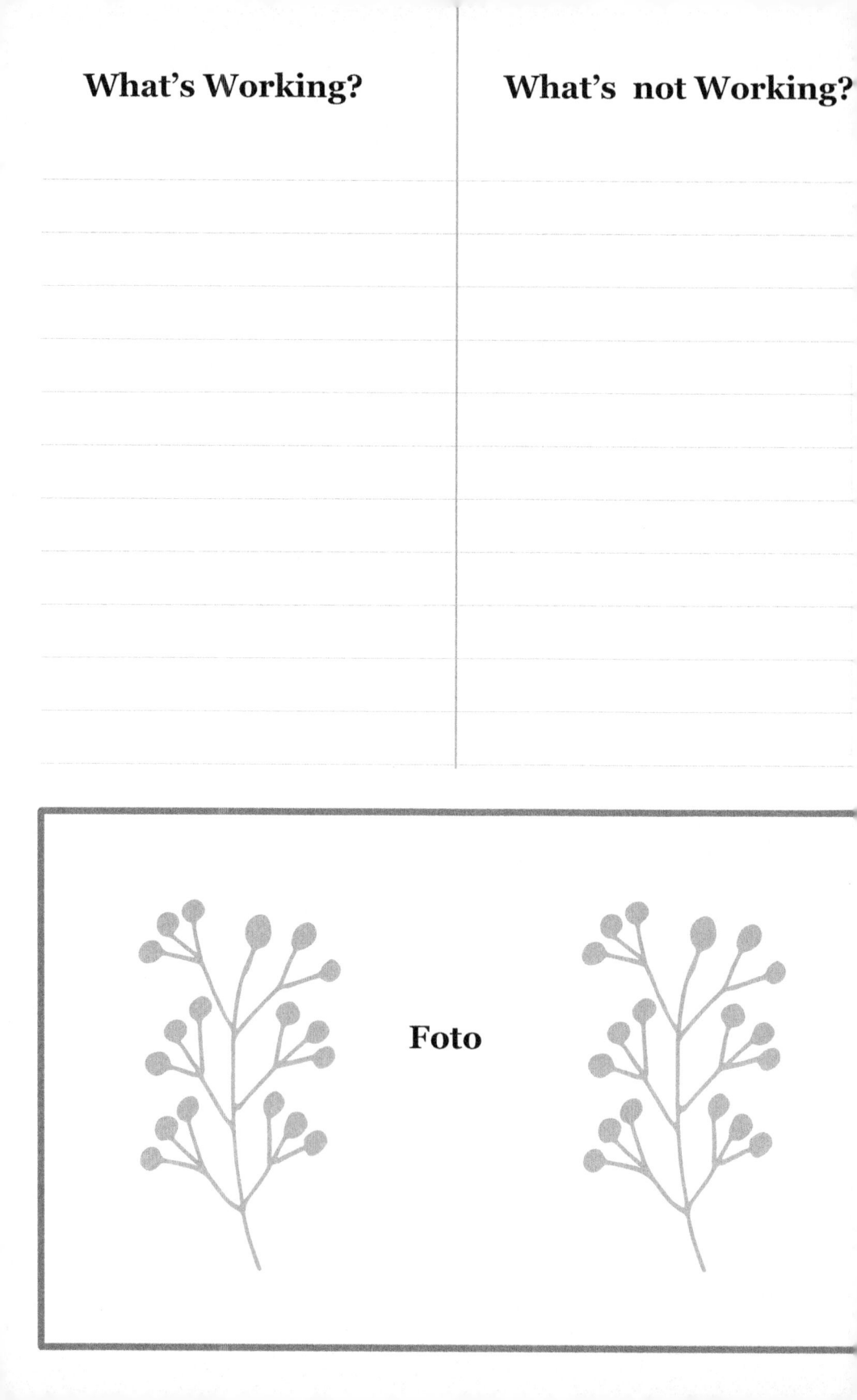

What's Working? | What's not Working?

Foto

Plant Name _____

Purchased At _____ Price _____

Date Planted _____ Harvested _____

Planted from   Seeds ☐   Transplant ☐

Plant Type

Fruit ○	Vegetable ○	Flower ○
Herb ○	Shrub ○	Tree ○
Seedling ○	Annual ○	Biennial ○
Perennial ○	Grass ○	Weed ○

Water Requirement   A little 💧   AVG 💧💧   A Lot 💧💧💧

Sunlight Needed   A little ☀   AVG ☀☀   A Lot ☀☀☀

Fertilizers Used

Rating   Notes

Size   ☆ ☆ ☆ ☆ ☆

Color ☆ ☆ ☆ ☆ ☆

Taste ☆ ☆ ☆ ☆ ☆

What's Working?	What's not Working?

Foto

Plant Name _____

Purchased At _____ Price _____

Date Planted _____ Harvested _____

Planted from   Seeds ☐   Transplant ☐

Plant Type

Fruit ○	Vegetable ○	Flower ○
Herb ○	Shrub ○	Tree ○
Seedling ○	Annual ○	Biennial ○
Perennial ○	Grass ○	Weed ○

Water Requirement   A little   AVG   A Lot

Sunlight Needed   A little   AVG   A Lot

Fertilizers Used _____

Rating   Notes

Size   ☆ ☆ ☆ ☆ ☆
Color ☆ ☆ ☆ ☆ ☆
Taste ☆ ☆ ☆ ☆ ☆

What's Working? | What's not Working?

Foto

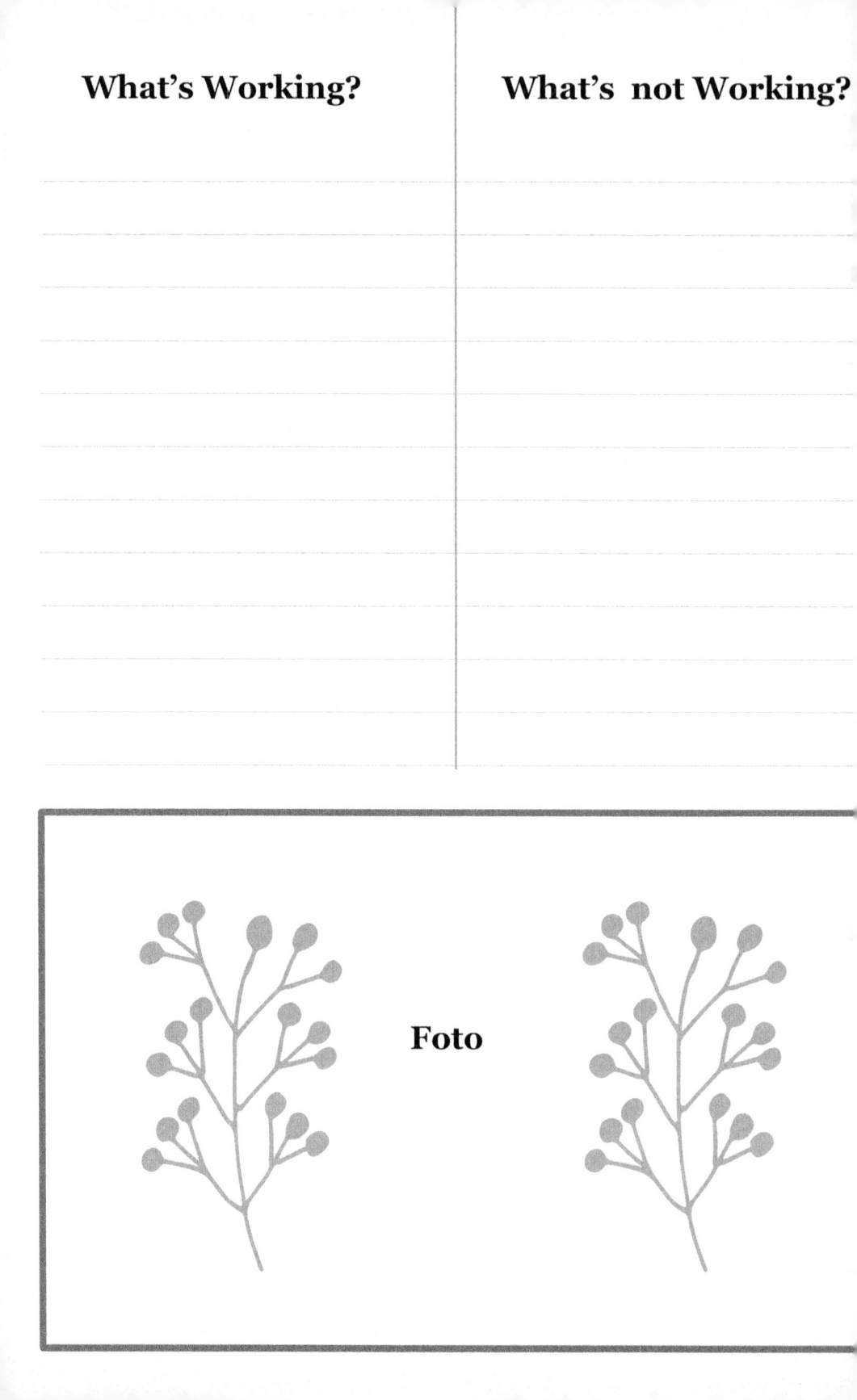

Plant Name _____

Purchased At _____ Price _____

Date Planted _____ Harvested _____

Planted from   Seeds ☐   Transplant ☐

Plant Type

Fruit ○	Vegetable ○	Flower ○
Herb ○	Shrub ○	Tree ○
Seedling ○	Annual ○	Biennial ○
Perennial ○	Grass ○	Weed ○

Water Requirement   A little   AVG   A Lot

Sunlight Needed   A little   AVG   A Lot

Fertilizers Used

Rating   Notes

Size   ☆ ☆ ☆ ☆ ☆

Color ☆ ☆ ☆ ☆ ☆

Taste ☆ ☆ ☆ ☆ ☆

What's Working?	What's not Working?

Foto

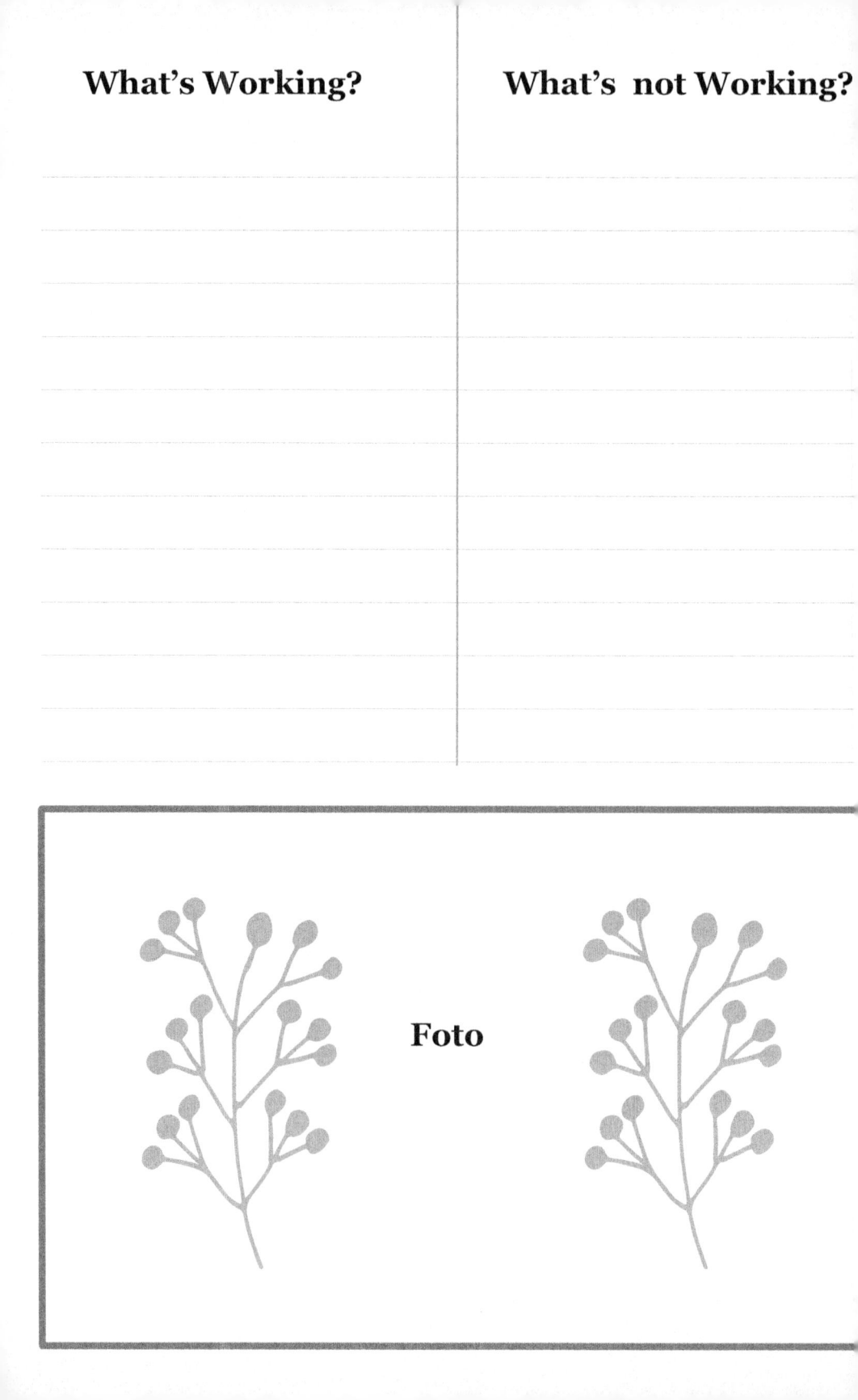

Plant Name _____

Purchased At _____ Price _____

Date Planted _____ Harvested _____

Planted from   Seeds ☐   Transplant ☐

Plant Type

Fruit ⚘	Vegetable ⚘	Flower ⚘
Herb ⚘	Shrub ⚘	Tree ⚘
Seedling ⚘	Annual ⚘	Biennial ⚘
Perennial ⚘	Grass ⚘	Weed ⚘

Water Requirement   A little 💧   AVG 💧💧   A Lot 💧💧💧

Sunlight Needed   A little ☀   AVG ☀☀   A Lot ☀☀☀

Fertilizers Used _____

Rating   Notes

Size   ☆ ☆ ☆ ☆ ☆

Color ☆ ☆ ☆ ☆ ☆

Taste ☆ ☆ ☆ ☆ ☆

What's Working?

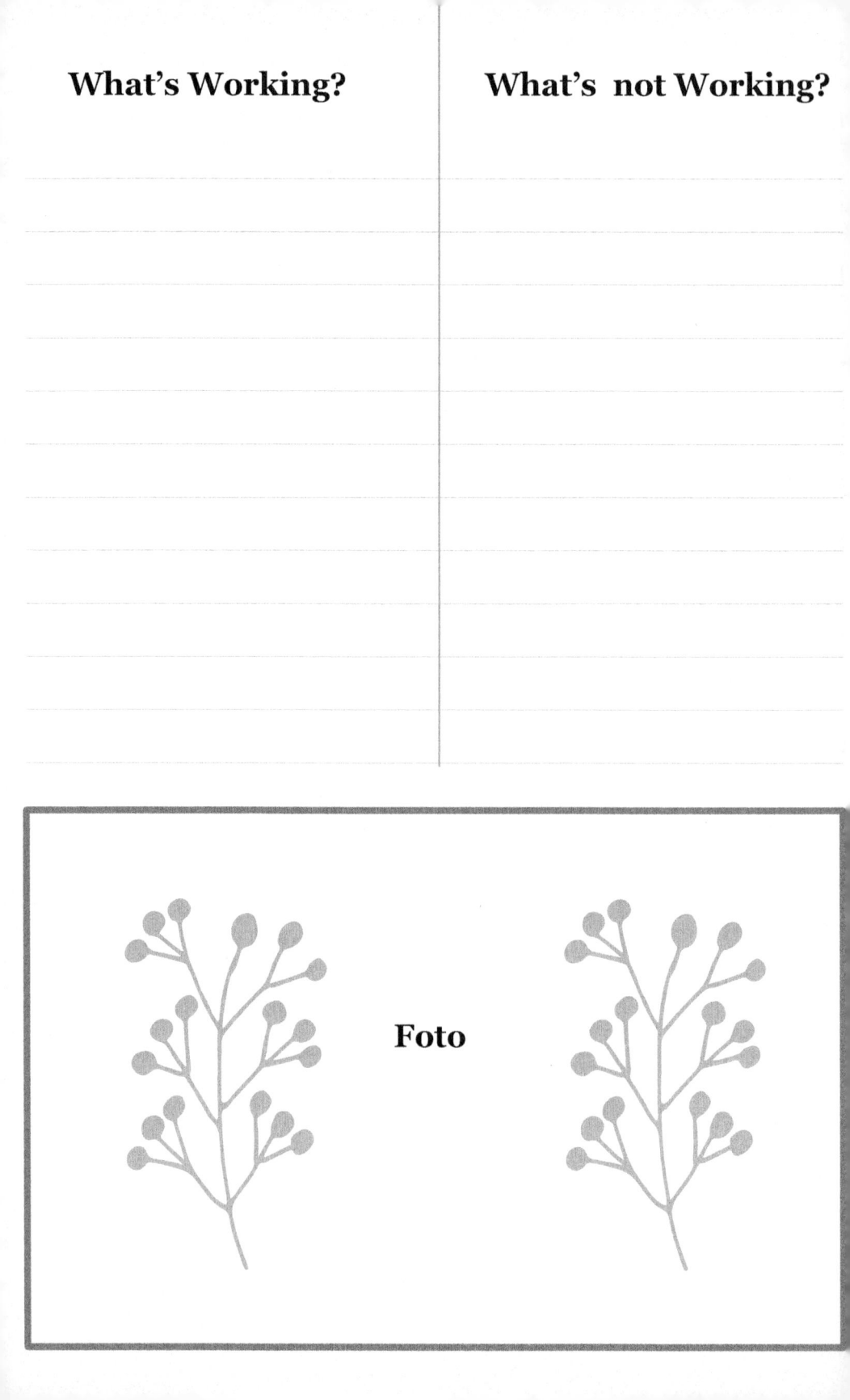

What's not Working?

Foto

Plant Name _____

Purchased At _____ Price _____

Date Planted _____ Harvested _____

Planted from   Seeds ☐   Transplant ☐

Plant Type

Fruit ⚬	Vegetable ⚬	Flower ⚬
Herb ⚬	Shrub ⚬	Tree ⚬
Seedling ⚬	Annual ⚬	Biennial ⚬
Perennial ⚬	Grass ⚬	Weed ⚬

Water Requirement   A little 💧   AVG 💧💧   A Lot 💧💧💧

Sunlight Needed   A little ☀   AVG ☀☀   A Lot ☀☀☀

Fertilizers Used

Rating   ## Notes

Size   ☆ ☆ ☆ ☆ ☆

Color ☆ ☆ ☆ ☆ ☆

Taste ☆ ☆ ☆ ☆ ☆

What's Working?	What's not Working?

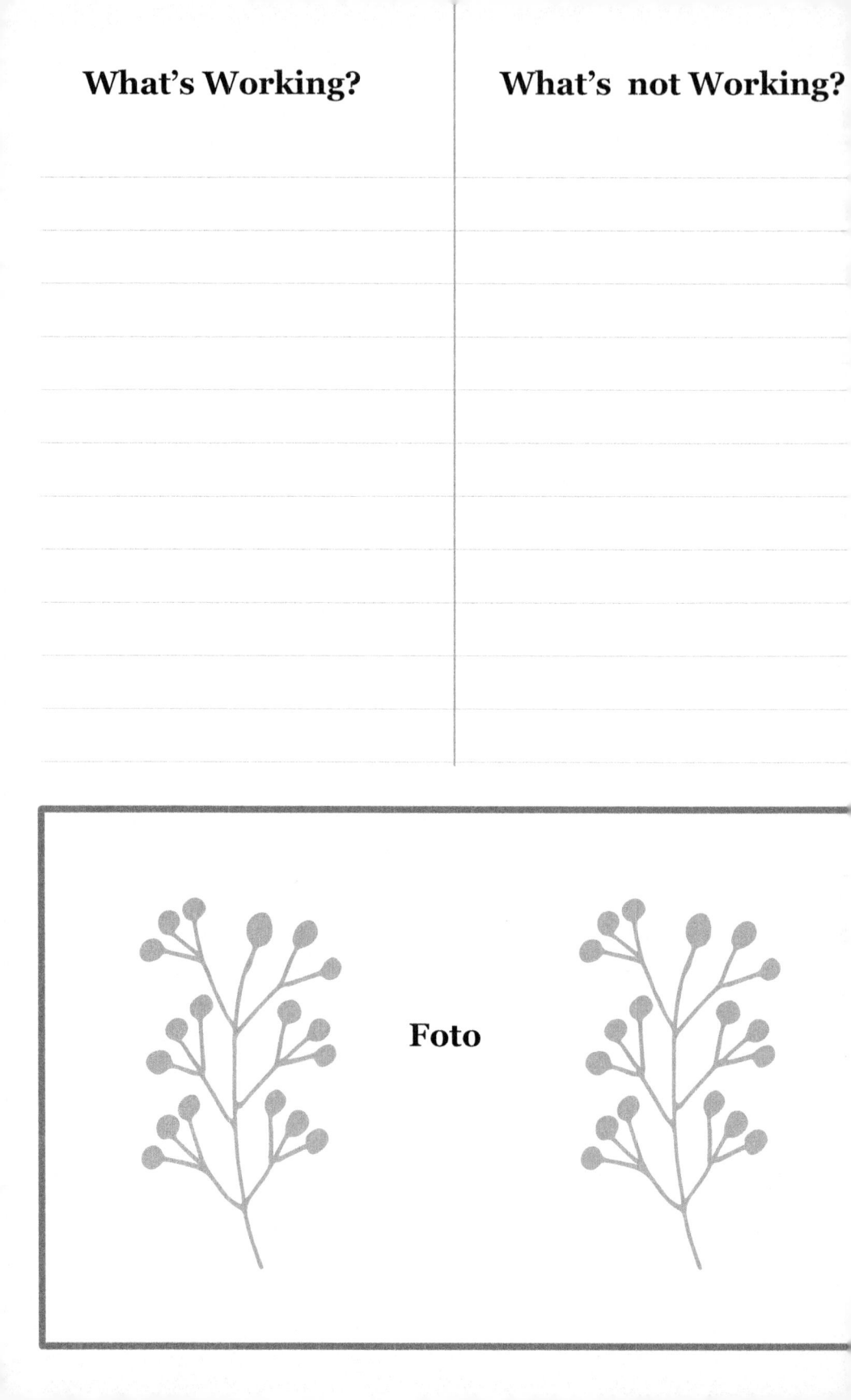

Foto

Plant Name _____

Purchased At _____ Price _____

Date Planted _____ Harvested _____

Planted from   Seeds ☐   Transplant ☐

Plant Type

Fruit	Vegetable	Flower
Herb	Shrub	Tree
Seedling	Annual	Biennial
Perennial	Grass	Weed

Water Requirement   A little   AVG   A Lot

Sunlight Needed   A little   AVG   A Lot

Fertilizers Used _____

Rating   ## Notes

Size   ☆ ☆ ☆ ☆ ☆
Color   ☆ ☆ ☆ ☆ ☆
Taste   ☆ ☆ ☆ ☆ ☆

What's Working?	What's not Working?

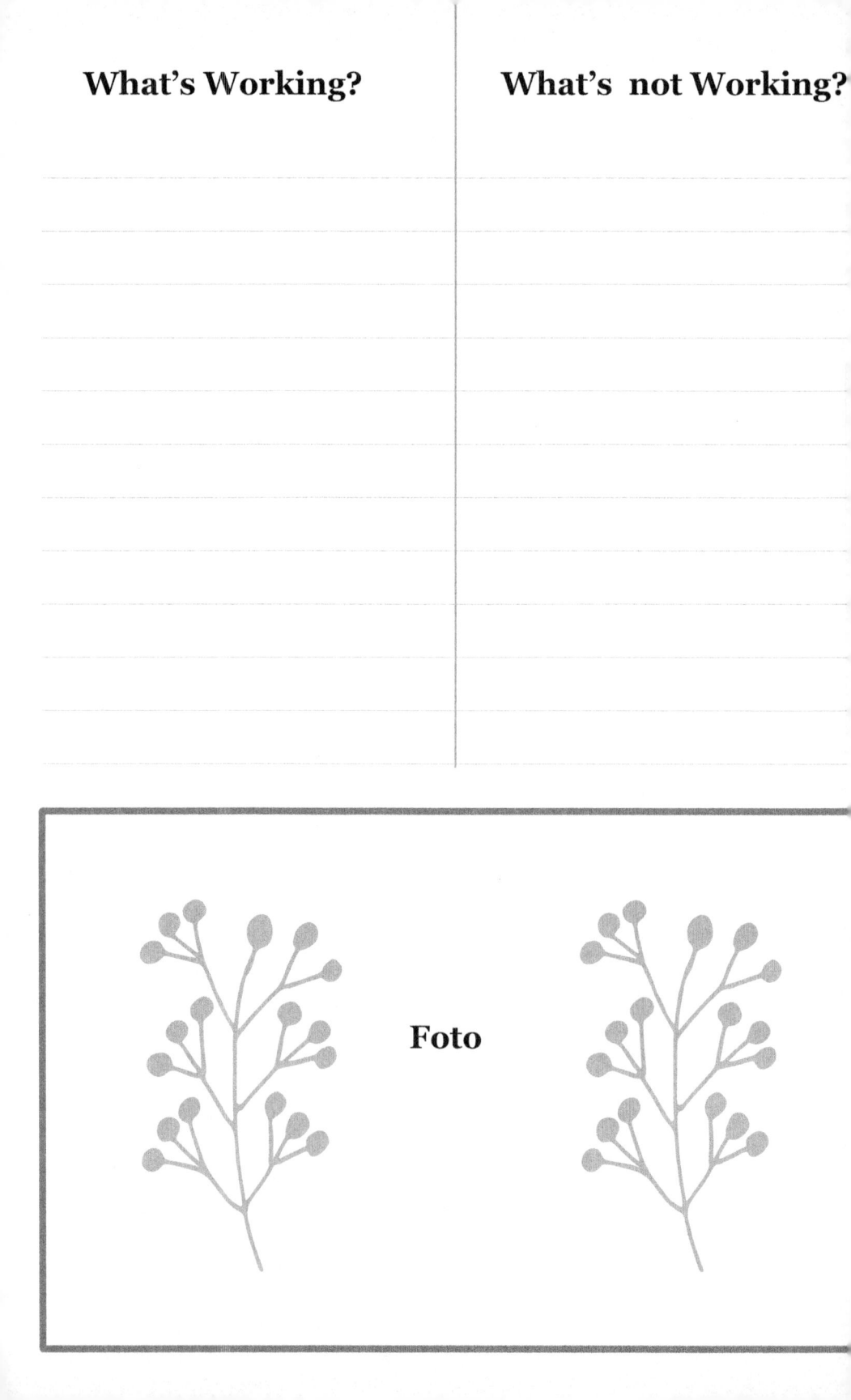

Foto

Plant Name _____

Purchased At _____ Price _____

Date Planted _____ Harvested _____

Planted from   Seeds ☐   Transplant ☐

Plant Type

Fruit ◯	Vegetable ◯	Flower ◯
Herb ◯	Shrub ◯	Tree ◯
Seedling ◯	Annual ◯	Biennial ◯
Perennial ◯	Grass ◯	Weed ◯

Water Requirement   A little 💧   AVG 💧💧   A Lot 💧💧💧

Sunlight Needed   A little ☼   AVG ☼☼   A Lot ☼☼☼☼

Fertilizers Used _____

Rating   Notes

Size   ☆ ☆ ☆ ☆ ☆
Color ☆ ☆ ☆ ☆ ☆
Taste ☆ ☆ ☆ ☆ ☆

What's Working?	What's not Working?

Foto

Plant Name _____

Purchased At _____ Price _____

Date Planted _____ Harvested _____

Planted from   Seeds ☐   Transplant ☐

Plant Type

Fruit	Vegetable	Flower
Herb	Shrub	Tree
Seedling	Annual	Biennial
Perennial	Grass	Weed

Water Requirement   A little   AVG   A Lot

Sunlight Needed   A little   AVG   A Lot

Fertilizers Used _____

Rating   Notes

Size   ☆ ☆ ☆ ☆ ☆

Color ☆ ☆ ☆ ☆ ☆

Taste ☆ ☆ ☆ ☆ ☆

What's Working?	What's not Working?

Foto

Plant Name _____

Purchased At _____ Price _____

Date Planted _____ Harvested _____

Planted from   Seeds ☐   Transplant ☐

Plant Type

Fruit	Vegetable	Flower
Herb	Shrub	Tree
Seedling	Annual	Biennial
Perennial	Grass	Weed

Water Requirement   A little   AVG   A Lot

Sunlight Needed   A little   AVG   A Lot

Fertilizers Used _____

Rating   Notes

Size ☆ ☆ ☆ ☆ ☆

Color ☆ ☆ ☆ ☆ ☆

Taste ☆ ☆ ☆ ☆ ☆

What's Working?

What's not Working?

Foto

Plant Name _____

Purchased At _____ Price _____

Date Planted _____ Harvested _____

Planted from   Seeds ☐   Transplant ☐

Plant Type

Fruit	Vegetable	Flower
Herb	Shrub	Tree
Seedling	Annual	Biennial
Perennial	Grass	Weed

Water Requirement   A little   AVG   A Lot

Sunlight Needed   A little   AVG   A Lot

Fertilizers Used _____

Rating   Notes

Size   ☆ ☆ ☆ ☆ ☆

Color   ☆ ☆ ☆ ☆ ☆

Taste   ☆ ☆ ☆ ☆ ☆

What's Working?	**What's not Working?**

Foto

Plant Name _____

Purchased At _____ Price _____

Date Planted _____ Harvested _____

Planted from   Seeds ☐   Transplant ☐

Plant Type

Fruit ○	Vegetable ○	Flower ○
Herb ○	Shrub ○	Tree ○
Seedling ○	Annual ○	Biennial ○
Perennial ○	Grass ○	Weed ○

Water Requirement   A little 💧   AVG 💧💧   A Lot 💧💧💧

Sunlight Needed   A little ☀   AVG ☀☀   A Lot ☀☀☀

Fertilizers Used _____

Rating   Notes

Size   ☆ ☆ ☆ ☆ ☆
Color   ☆ ☆ ☆ ☆ ☆
Taste   ☆ ☆ ☆ ☆ ☆

What's Working? | What's not Working?

Foto

Plant Name _____

Purchased At _____ Price _____

Date Planted _____ Harvested _____

Planted from   Seeds ☐   Transplant ☐

Plant Type

Fruit ❀	Vegetable ❀	Flower ❀
Herb ❀	Shrub ❀	Tree ❀
Seedling ❀	Annual ❀	Biennial ❀
Perennial ❀	Grass ❀	Weed ❀

Water Requirement   A little 💧   AVG 💧💧   A Lot 💧💧💧

Sunlight Needed   A little ☀   AVG ☀☀   A Lot ☀☀☀

Fertilizers Used _____

Rating   ## Notes

Size   ☆ ☆ ☆ ☆ ☆

Color ☆ ☆ ☆ ☆ ☆

Taste ☆ ☆ ☆ ☆ ☆

What's Working?	What's not Working?

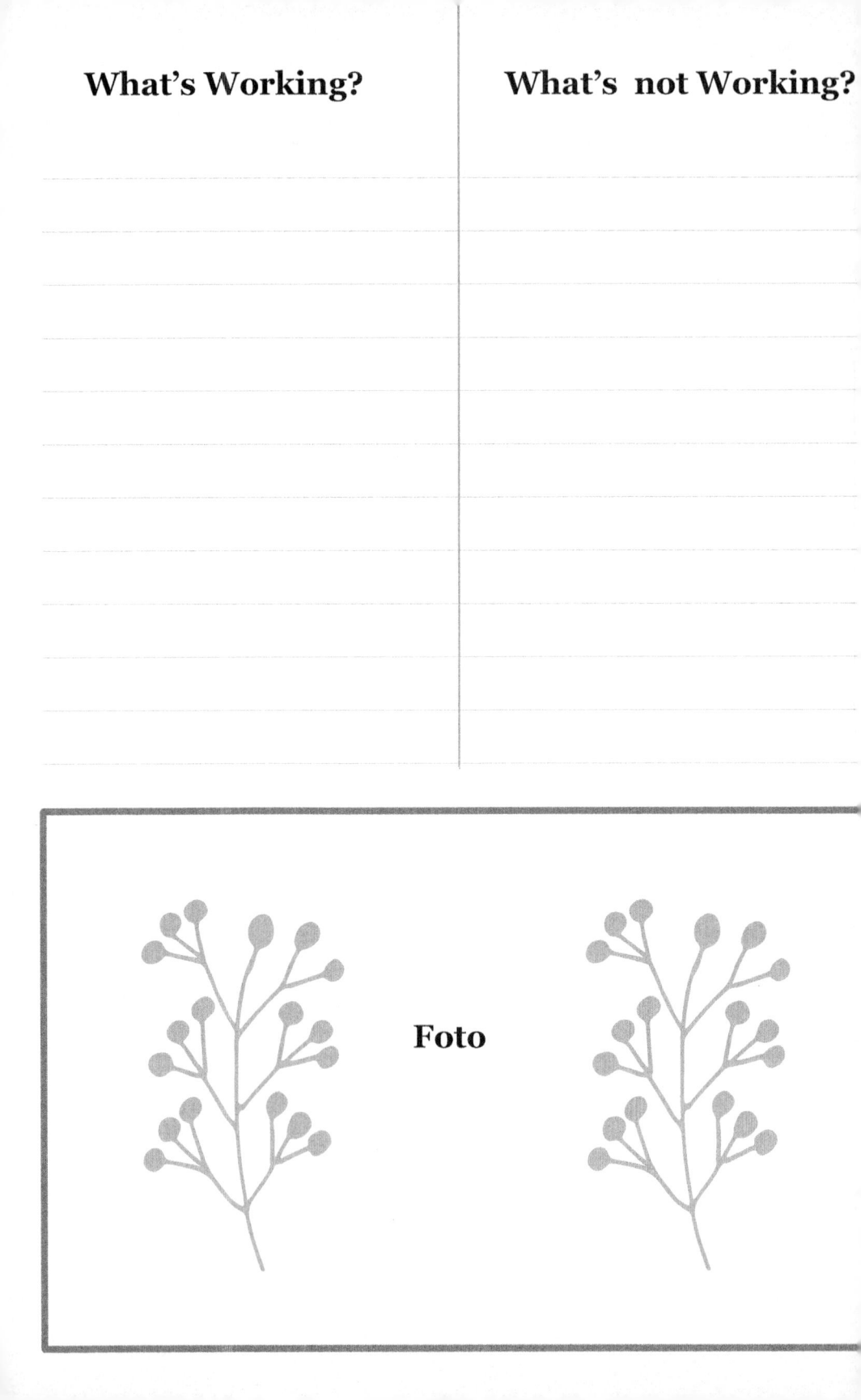

Foto

Plant Name _____

Purchased At _____ Price _____

Date Planted _____ Harvested _____

Planted from   Seeds ☐   Transplant ☐

Plant Type

Fruit ○	Vegetable ○	Flower ○
Herb ○	Shrub ○	Tree ○
Seedling ○	Annual ○	Biennial ○
Perennial ○	Grass ○	Weed ○

Water Requirement   A little 💧   AVG 💧💧   A Lot 💧💧💧

Sunlight Needed   A little ☀   AVG ☀☀   A Lot ☀☀☀

Fertilizers Used _____

Rating   ## Notes

Size   ☆ ☆ ☆ ☆ ☆

Color ☆ ☆ ☆ ☆ ☆

Taste ☆ ☆ ☆ ☆ ☆

What's Working?	What's not Working?

Foto

Plant Name _____

Purchased At _____ Price _____

Date Planted _____ Harvested _____

Planted from   Seeds ☐   Transplant ☐

Plant Type

Fruit	Vegetable	Flower
Herb	Shrub	Tree
Seedling	Annual	Biennial
Perennial	Grass	Weed

Water Requirement   A little   AVG   A Lot

Sunlight Needed   A little   AVG   A Lot

Fertilizers Used _____

Rating   Notes

Size   ☆ ☆ ☆ ☆ ☆

Color ☆ ☆ ☆ ☆ ☆

Taste ☆ ☆ ☆ ☆ ☆

What's Working?

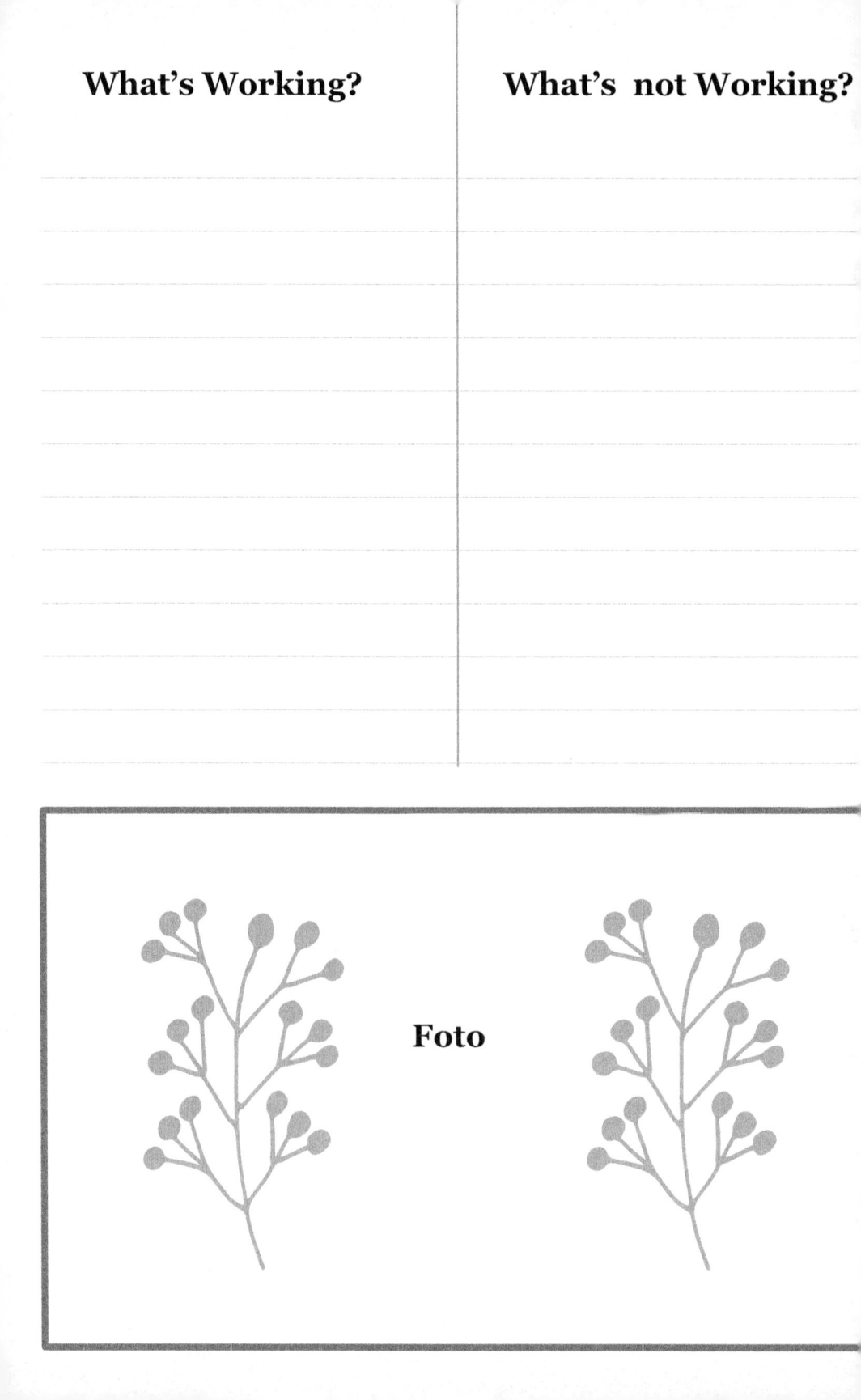

What's not Working?

Foto

Plant Name _____

Purchased At _____   Price _____

Date Planted _____   Harvested _____

Planted from   Seeds ☐   Transplant ☐

Plant Type

Fruit ✿	Vegetable ✿	Flower ✿
Herb ✿	Shrub ✿	Tree ✿
Seedling ✿	Annual ✿	Biennial ✿
Perennial ✿	Grass ✿	Weed ✿

Water Requirement   A little 💧   AVG 💧💧   A Lot 💧💧💧

Sunlight Needed   A little ☀   AVG ☀☀   A Lot ☀☀☀

Fertilizers Used _____

Rating   ## Notes

Size   ☆ ☆ ☆ ☆ ☆

Color   ☆ ☆ ☆ ☆ ☆

Taste   ☆ ☆ ☆ ☆ ☆

What's Working? | What's not Working?

Foto

Plant Name _____

Purchased At _____ Price _____

Date Planted _____ Harvested _____

Planted from   Seeds ☐   Transplant ☐

Plant Type

Fruit	Vegetable	Flower
Herb	Shrub	Tree
Seedling	Annual	Biennial
Perennial	Grass	Weed

Water Requirement   A little   AVG   A Lot

Sunlight Needed   A little   AVG   A Lot

Fertilizers Used

Rating   Notes

Size   ☆ ☆ ☆ ☆ ☆
Color   ☆ ☆ ☆ ☆ ☆
Taste   ☆ ☆ ☆ ☆ ☆

What's Working? | What's not Working?

Foto

Plant Name _____

Purchased At _____   Price _____

Date Planted _____   Harvested _____

Planted from   Seeds ☐   Transplant ☐

Plant Type

Fruit ⚪	Vegetable ⚪	Flower ⚪
Herb ⚪	Shrub ⚪	Tree ⚪
Seedling ⚪	Annual ⚪	Biennial ⚪
Perennial ⚪	Grass ⚪	Weed ⚪

Water Requirement   A little 💧   AVG 💧💧   A Lot 💧💧💧

Sunlight Needed   A little ☀   AVG ☀☀   A Lot ☀☀☀

Fertilizers Used _____

Rating   ## Notes

Size   ☆ ☆ ☆ ☆ ☆

Color   ☆ ☆ ☆ ☆ ☆

Taste   ☆ ☆ ☆ ☆ ☆

What's Working?	**What's not Working?**

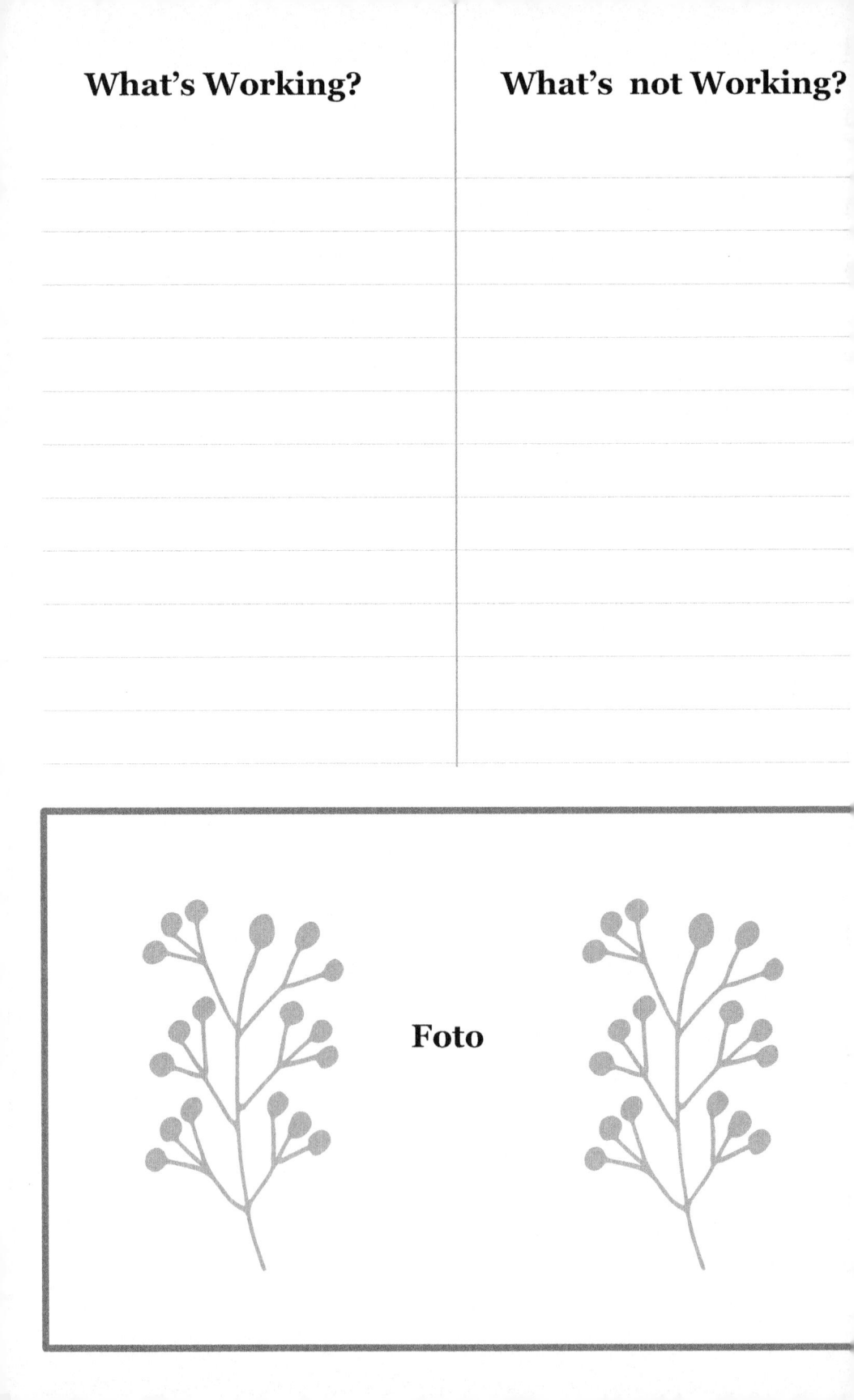

Foto

Plant Name _____

Purchased At _____ Price _____

Date Planted _____ Harvested _____

Planted from   Seeds ☐   Transplant ☐

Plant Type

Fruit ❀	Vegetable ❀	Flower ❀
Herb ❀	Shrub ❀	Tree ❀
Seedling ❀	Annual ❀	Biennial ❀
Perennial ❀	Grass ❀	Weed ❀

Water Requirement A little 💧   AVG 💧💧   A Lot 💧💧💧

Sunlight Needed A little ☀   AVG ☀☀   A Lot ☀☀☀

Fertilizers Used _____

Rating   ## Notes

Size ☆ ☆ ☆ ☆ ☆
Color ☆ ☆ ☆ ☆ ☆
Taste ☆ ☆ ☆ ☆ ☆

What's Working?

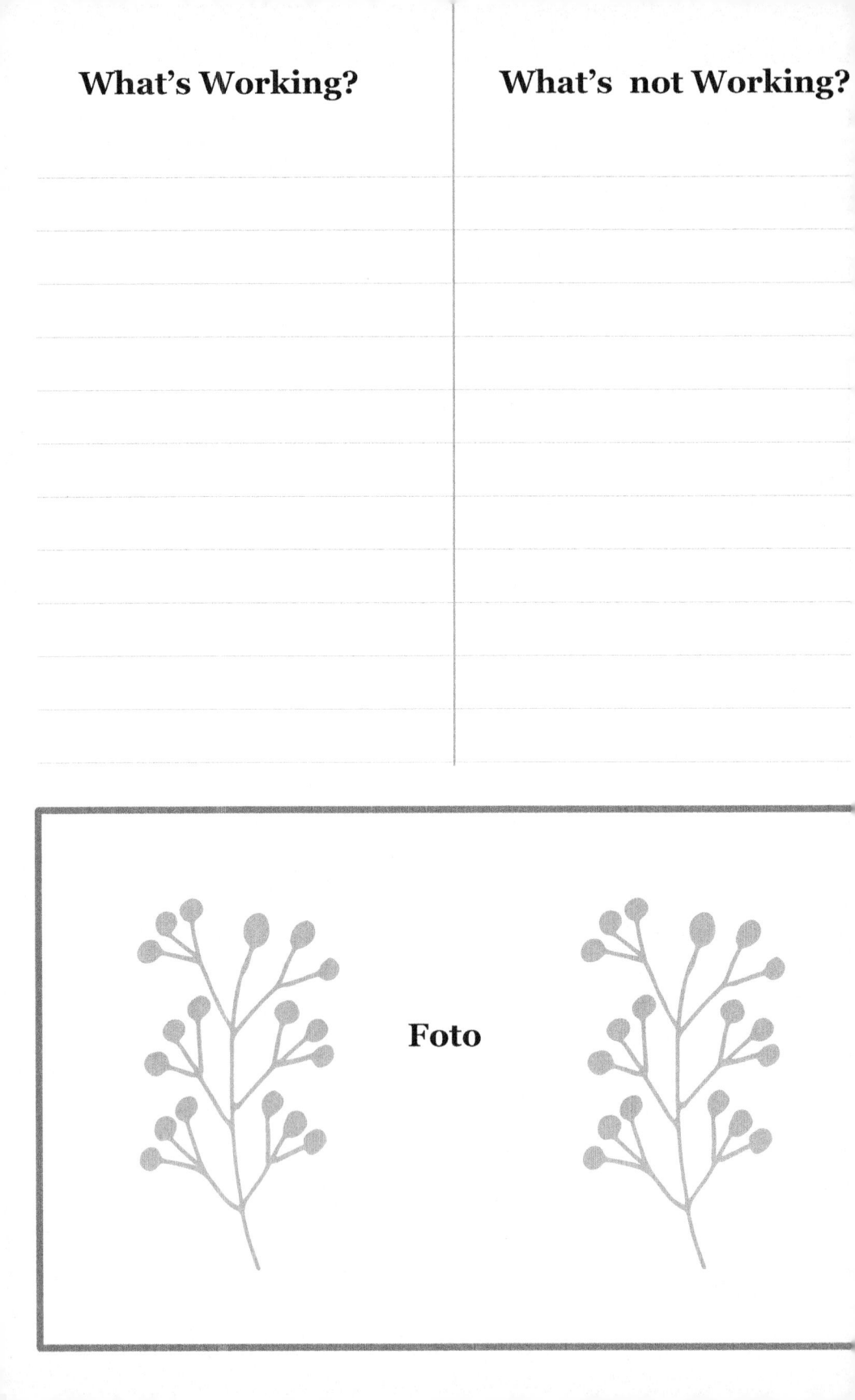

What's not Working?

Foto

Plant Name _____

Purchased At _____ Price _____

Date Planted _____ Harvested _____

Planted from   Seeds ☐   Transplant ☐

Plant Type

Fruit	Vegetable	Flower
Herb	Shrub	Tree
Seedling	Annual	Biennial
Perennial	Grass	Weed

Water Requirement   A little   AVG   A Lot

Sunlight Needed   A little   AVG   A Lot

Fertilizers Used _____

Rating   Notes

Size   ☆ ☆ ☆ ☆ ☆

Color   ☆ ☆ ☆ ☆ ☆

Taste   ☆ ☆ ☆ ☆ ☆

What's Working?

What's not Working?

Foto

Plant Name _____

Purchased At _____ Price _____

Date Planted _____ Harvested _____

Planted from   Seeds ☐   Transplant ☐

Plant Type

Fruit ✿	Vegetable ✿	Flower ✿
Herb ✿	Shrub ✿	Tree ✿
Seedling ✿	Annual ✿	Biennial ✿
Perennial ✿	Grass ✿	Weed ✿

Water Requirement   A little 💧   AVG 💧💧   A Lot 💧💧💧

Sunlight Needed   A little ☀   AVG ☀☀   A Lot ☀☀☀

Fertilizers Used

Rating   ## Notes

Size   ☆ ☆ ☆ ☆ ☆

Color   ☆ ☆ ☆ ☆ ☆

Taste   ☆ ☆ ☆ ☆ ☆

What's Working?	What's not Working?

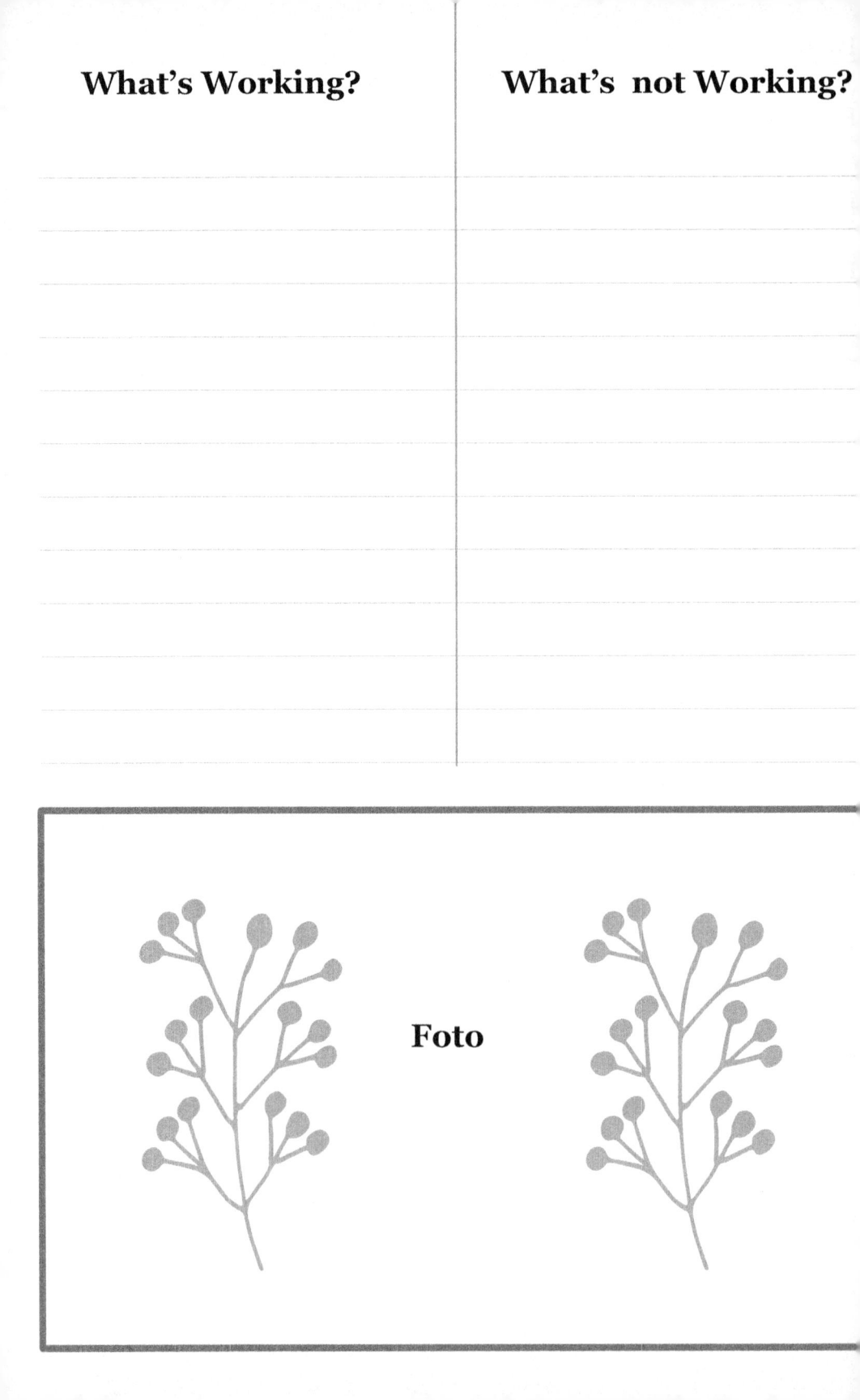

Foto

Plant Name _____

Purchased At _____ Price _____

Date Planted _____ Harvested _____

Planted from   Seeds ☐   Transplant ☐

Plant Type

Fruit ○	Vegetable ○	Flower ○
Herb ○	Shrub ○	Tree ○
Seedling ○	Annual ○	Biennial ○
Perennial ○	Grass ○	Weed ○

Water Requirement   A little 💧   AVG 💧💧   A Lot 💧💧💧

Sunlight Needed   A little ☼   AVG ☼☼   A Lot ☼☼☼

Fertilizers Used _____

Rating   Notes

Size   ☆ ☆ ☆ ☆ ☆

Color ☆ ☆ ☆ ☆ ☆

Taste ☆ ☆ ☆ ☆ ☆

What's Working? | What's not Working?

Foto

Plant Name _____

Purchased At _____ Price _____

Date Planted _____ Harvested _____

Planted from   Seeds ☐   Transplant ☐

Plant Type

Fruit	Vegetable	Flower
Herb	Shrub	Tree
Seedling	Annual	Biennial
Perennial	Grass	Weed

Water Requirement   A little   AVG   A Lot

Sunlight Needed   A little   AVG   A Lot

Fertilizers Used

Rating   Notes

Size   ☆ ☆ ☆ ☆ ☆
Color   ☆ ☆ ☆ ☆ ☆
Taste   ☆ ☆ ☆ ☆ ☆

What's Working? | What's not Working?

Foto

Plant Name _____

Purchased At _____ Price _____

Date Planted _____ Harvested _____

Planted from   Seeds ☐   Transplant ☐

Plant Type

Fruit ✿	Vegetable ✿	Flower ✿
Herb ✿	Shrub ✿	Tree ✿
Seedling ✿	Annual ✿	Biennial ✿
Perennial ✿	Grass ✿	Weed ✿

Water Requirement   A little 💧   AVG 💧💧   A Lot 💧💧💧

Sunlight Needed   A little ☼   AVG ☼☼   A Lot ☼☼☼

Fertilizers Used _____

Rating   ## Notes

Size   ☆ ☆ ☆ ☆ ☆
Color ☆ ☆ ☆ ☆ ☆
Taste ☆ ☆ ☆ ☆ ☆

What's Working?	What's not Working?

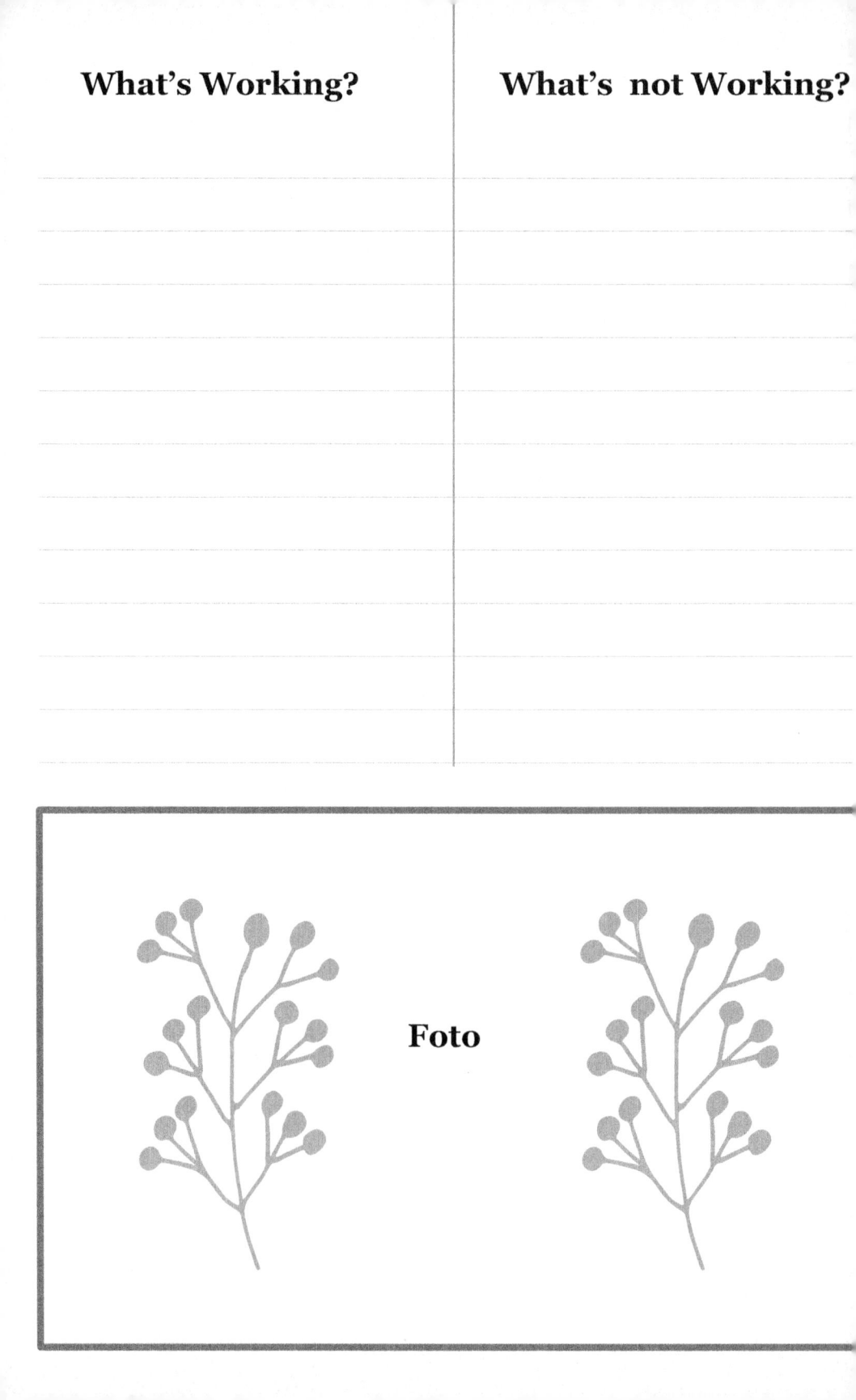

Foto

Plant Name _____

Purchased At _____ Price _____

Date Planted _____ Harvested _____

Planted from   Seeds ☐   Transplant ☐

Plant Type

Fruit ◯	Vegetable ◯	Flower ◯
Herb ◯	Shrub ◯	Tree ◯
Seedling ◯	Annual ◯	Biennial ◯
Perennial ◯	Grass ◯	Weed ◯

Water Requirement   A little 💧   AVG 💧💧   A Lot 💧💧💧

Sunlight Needed   A little ☀   AVG ☀☀   A Lot ☀☀☀

Fertilizers Used _____

Rating   ## Notes

Size   ☆ ☆ ☆ ☆ ☆

Color   ☆ ☆ ☆ ☆ ☆

Taste   ☆ ☆ ☆ ☆ ☆

What's Working? | What's not Working?

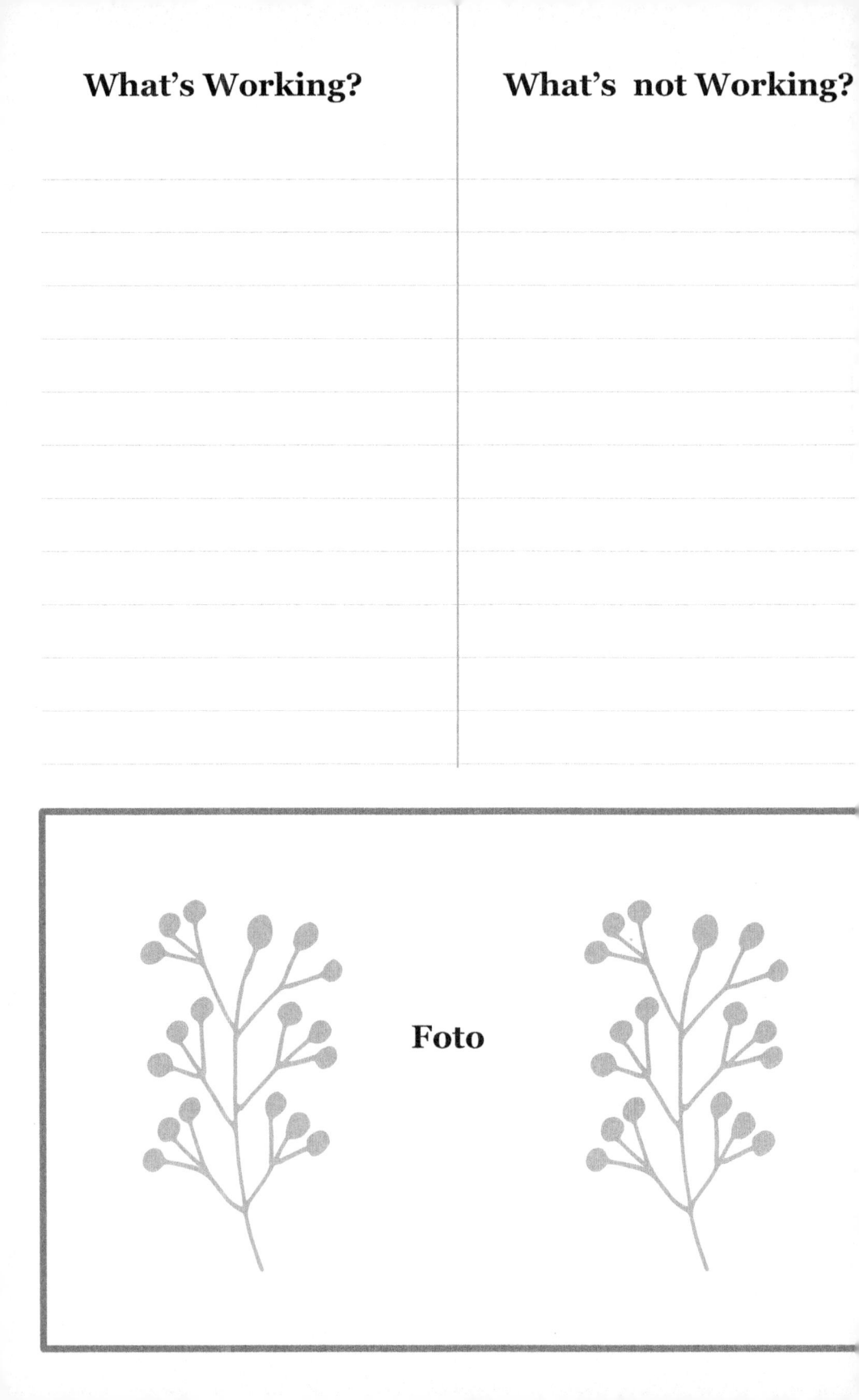

Foto

Plant Name _____

Purchased At _____ Price _____

Date Planted _____ Harvested _____

Planted from   Seeds ☐   Transplant ☐

Plant Type

Fruit	Vegetable	Flower
Herb	Shrub	Tree
Seedling	Annual	Biennial
Perennial	Grass	Weed

Water Requirement   A little   AVG   A Lot

Sunlight Needed   A little   AVG   A Lot

Fertilizers Used _____

Rating   Notes

Size ☆ ☆ ☆ ☆ ☆
Color ☆ ☆ ☆ ☆ ☆
Taste ☆ ☆ ☆ ☆ ☆

What's Working?

What's not Working?

Foto

Plant Name _____

Purchased At _____ Price _____

Date Planted _____ Harvested _____

Planted from   Seeds ☐   Transplant ☐

Plant Type

Fruit ❀	Vegetable ❀	Flower ❀
Herb ❀	Shrub ❀	Tree ❀
Seedling ❀	Annual ❀	Biennial ❀
Perennial ❀	Grass ❀	Weed ❀

Water Requirement   A little 💧   AVG 💧💧   A Lot 💧💧💧

Sunlight Needed   A little ✲   AVG ✲✲   A Lot ✲✲✲

Fertilizers Used _____

Rating   ## Notes

Size   ☆ ☆ ☆ ☆ ☆

Color ☆ ☆ ☆ ☆ ☆

Taste ☆ ☆ ☆ ☆ ☆

What's Working?	What's not Working?

Foto

Plant Name _____

Purchased At _____ Price _____

Date Planted _____ Harvested _____

Planted from   Seeds ☐   Transplant ☐

Plant Type

Fruit ⬡	Vegetable ⬡	Flower ⬡
Herb ⬡	Shrub ⬡	Tree ⬡
Seedling ⬡	Annual ⬡	Biennial ⬡
Perennial ⬡	Grass ⬡	Weed ⬡

Water Requirement   A little 💧   AVG 💧💧   A Lot 💧💧💧

Sunlight Needed   A little ☀   AVG ☀☀   A Lot ☀☀☀

Fertilizers Used _____

Rating   ## Notes

Size   ☆ ☆ ☆ ☆ ☆
Color   ☆ ☆ ☆ ☆ ☆
Taste   ☆ ☆ ☆ ☆ ☆

What's Working?　　What's not Working?

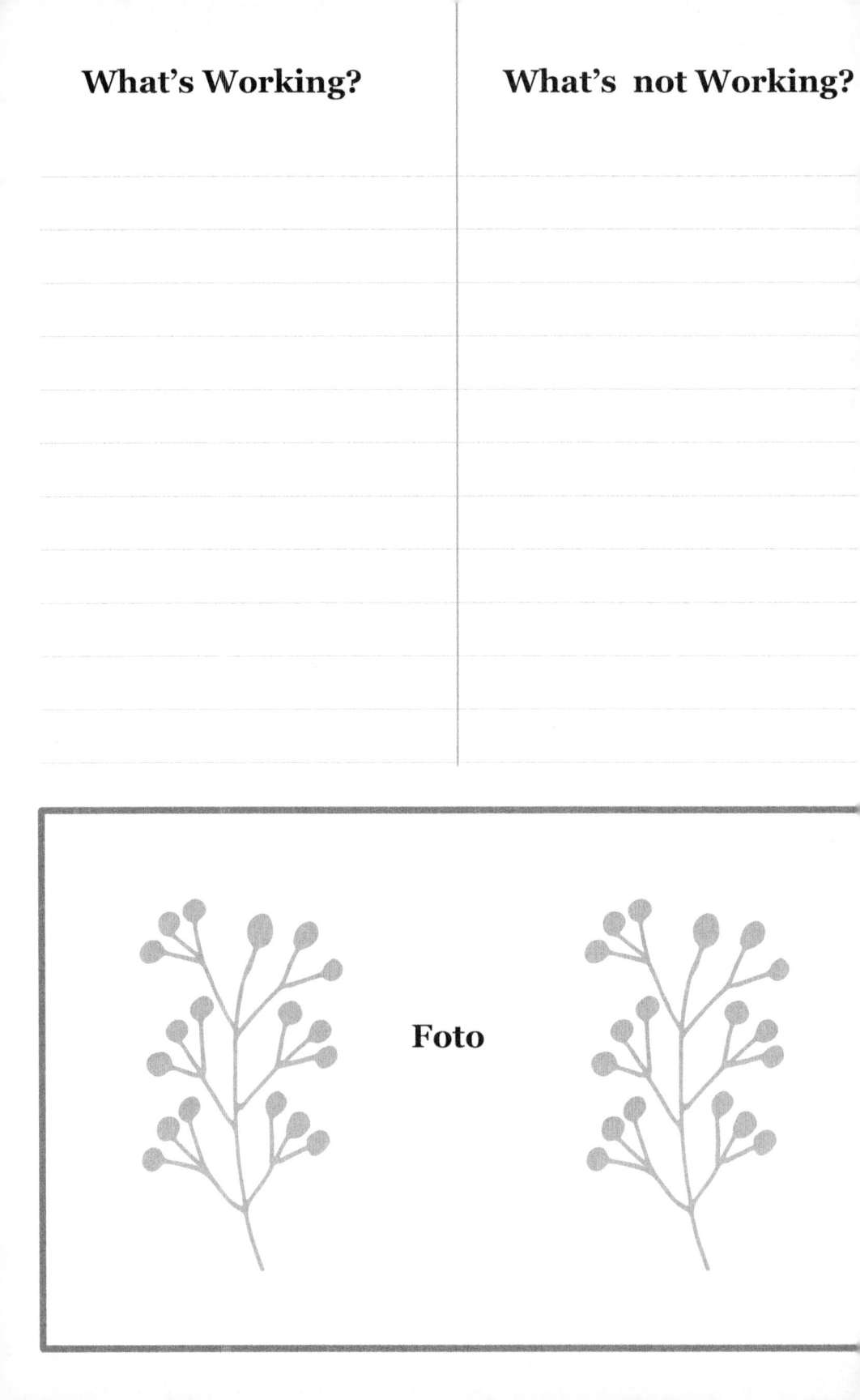

Foto

Plant Name _____

Purchased At _____   Price _____

Date Planted _____   Harvested _____

Planted from   Seeds ☐   Transplant ☐

Plant Type

Fruit ○	Vegetable ○	Flower ○
Herb ○	Shrub ○	Tree ○
Seedling ○	Annual ○	Biennial ○
Perennial ○	Grass ○	Weed ○

Water Requirement   A little 💧   AVG 💧💧   A Lot 💧💧💧

Sunlight Needed   A little ☀   AVG ☀☀   A Lot ☀☀☀

Fertilizers Used _____

Rating   ## Notes

Size   ☆ ☆ ☆ ☆ ☆

Color   ☆ ☆ ☆ ☆ ☆

Taste   ☆ ☆ ☆ ☆ ☆

What's Working?	What's not Working?

Foto

Plant Name _____

Purchased At _____ Price _____

Date Planted _____ Harvested _____

Planted from   Seeds ☐   Transplant ☐

Plant Type

Fruit ○	Vegetable ○	Flower ○
Herb ○	Shrub ○	Tree ○
Seedling ○	Annual ○	Biennial ○
Perennial ○	Grass ○	Weed ○

Water Requirement   A little 💧   AVG 💧💧   A Lot 💧💧💧

Sunlight Needed   A little ☀   AVG ☀☀   A Lot ☀☀☀

Fertilizers Used _____

Rating   ## Notes

Size   ☆ ☆ ☆ ☆ ☆

Color ☆ ☆ ☆ ☆ ☆

Taste ☆ ☆ ☆ ☆ ☆

What's Working?	**What's not Working?**

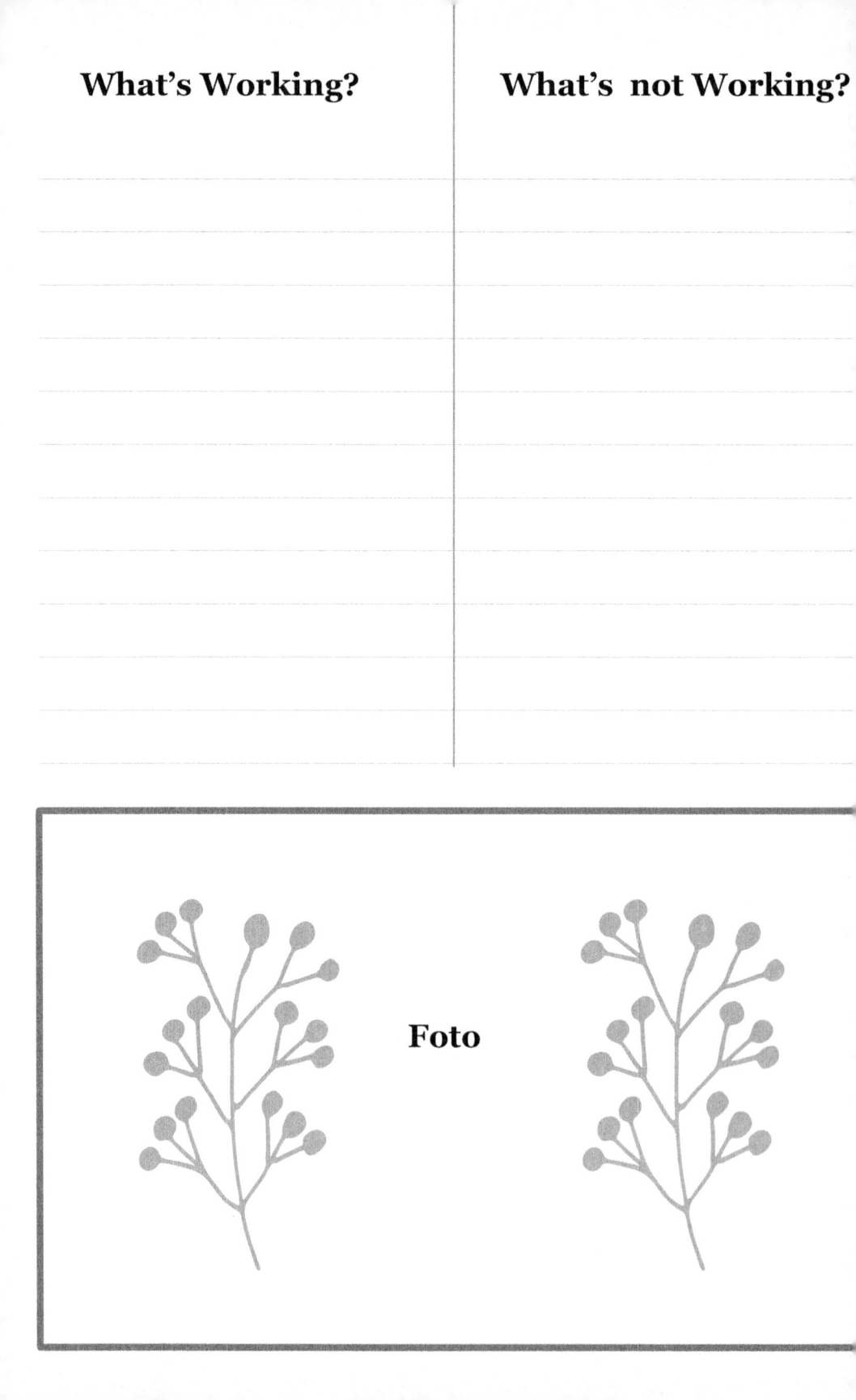

Foto

Plant Name _____

Purchased At _____ Price _____

Date Planted _____ Harvested _____

Planted from   Seeds ☐   Transplant ☐

Plant Type

Fruit ○	Vegetable ○	Flower ○
Herb ○	Shrub ○	Tree ○
Seedling ○	Annual ○	Biennial ○
Perennial ○	Grass ○	Weed ○

Water Requirement   A little 💧   AVG 💧💧   A Lot 💧💧💧

Sunlight Needed   A little ☀   AVG ☀☀   A Lot ☀☀☀

Fertilizers Used _____

Rating   ## Notes

Size   ☆ ☆ ☆ ☆ ☆

Color ☆ ☆ ☆ ☆ ☆

Taste ☆ ☆ ☆ ☆ ☆

What's Working? | What's not Working?

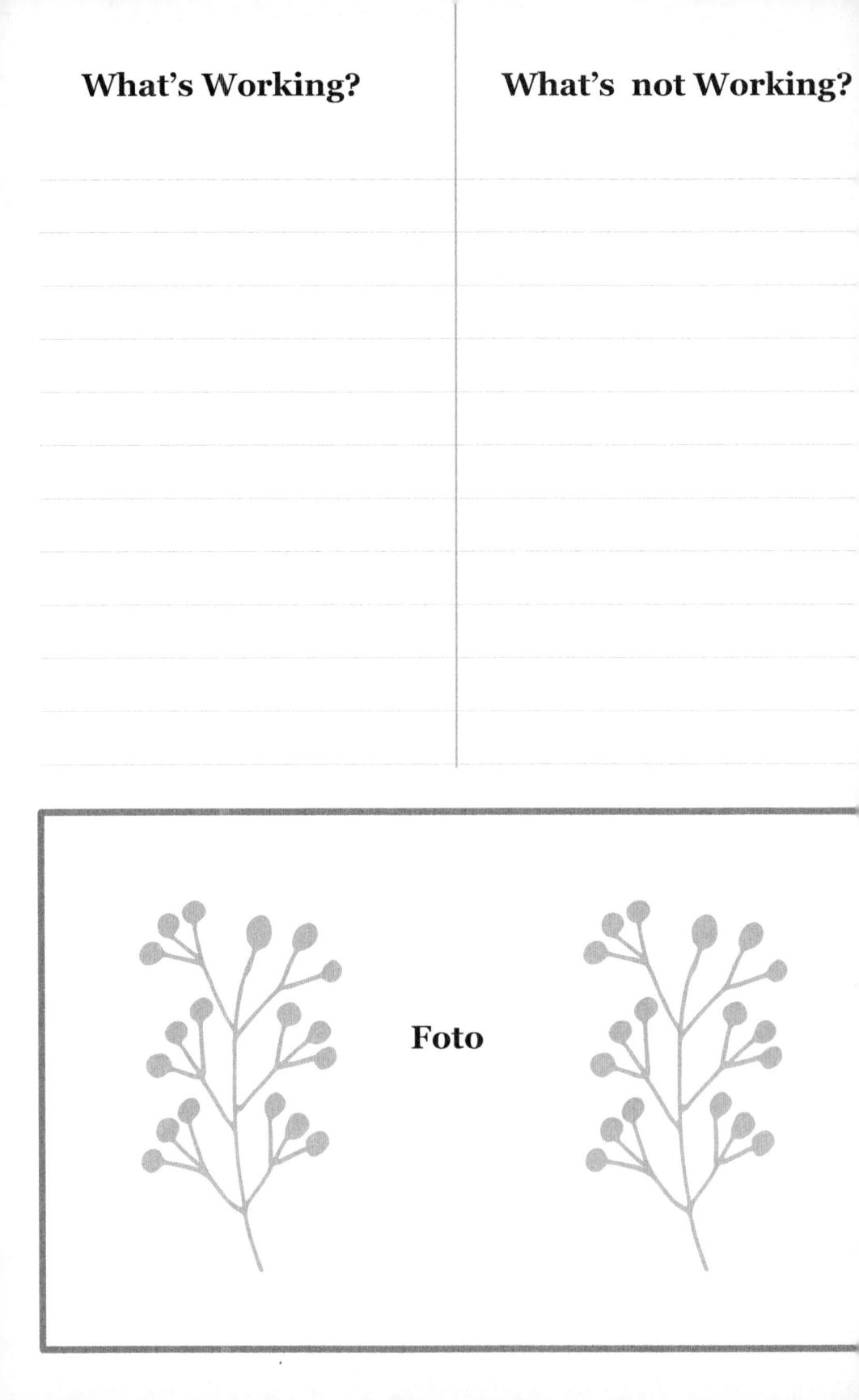

Foto

Plant Name _____

Purchased At _____ Price _____

Date Planted _____ Harvested _____

Planted from   Seeds ☐   Transplant ☐

Plant Type

Fruit ❀	Vegetable ❀	Flower ❀
Herb ❀	Shrub ❀	Tree ❀
Seedling ❀	Annual ❀	Biennial ❀
Perennial ❀	Grass ❀	Weed ❀

Water Requirement   A little 💧   AVG 💧💧   A Lot 💧💧💧

Sunlight Needed   A little ☀   AVG ☀☀   A Lot ☀☀☀

Fertilizers Used _____

Rating   Notes

Size   ☆ ☆ ☆ ☆ ☆
Color ☆ ☆ ☆ ☆ ☆
Taste ☆ ☆ ☆ ☆ ☆

What's Working? | What's not Working?

Foto

Plant Name _____

Purchased At _____ Price _____

Date Planted _____ Harvested _____

Planted from   Seeds ☐   Transplant ☐

Plant Type

Fruit ⚪	Vegetable ⚪	Flower ⚪
Herb ⚪	Shrub ⚪	Tree ⚪
Seedling ⚪	Annual ⚪	Biennial ⚪
Perennial ⚪	Grass ⚪	Weed ⚪

Water Requirement   A little   AVG   A Lot

Sunlight Needed   A little   AVG   A Lot

Fertilizers Used _____

Rating   ## Notes

Size   ☆ ☆ ☆ ☆ ☆

Color ☆ ☆ ☆ ☆ ☆

Taste ☆ ☆ ☆ ☆ ☆

What's Working?	What's not Working?

Foto

Plant Name _____

Purchased At _____ Price _____

Date Planted _____ Harvested _____

Planted from   Seeds ☐   Transplant ☐

Plant Type

Fruit ○	Vegetable ○	Flower ○
Herb ○	Shrub ○	Tree ○
Seedling ○	Annual ○	Biennial ○
Perennial ○	Grass ○	Weed ○

Water Requirement   A little 💧   AVG 💧💧   A Lot 💧💧💧

Sunlight Needed   A little ☀   AVG ☀☀   A Lot ☀☀☀

Fertilizers Used _____

Rating   ## Notes

Size   ☆ ☆ ☆ ☆ ☆

Color ☆ ☆ ☆ ☆ ☆

Taste ☆ ☆ ☆ ☆ ☆

What's Working?	What's not Working?

Foto

Plant Name _____

Purchased At _____ Price _____

Date Planted _____ Harvested _____

Planted from   Seeds ☐   Transplant ☐

Plant Type

Fruit	Vegetable	Flower
Herb	Shrub	Tree
Seedling	Annual	Biennial
Perennial	Grass	Weed

Water Requirement   A little   AVG   A Lot

Sunlight Needed   A little   AVG   A Lot

Fertilizers Used _____

Rating   Notes

Size   ☆ ☆ ☆ ☆ ☆
Color ☆ ☆ ☆ ☆ ☆
Taste ☆ ☆ ☆ ☆ ☆

What's Working?	What's not Working?

Foto

Plant Name _____

Purchased At _____   Price _____

Date Planted _____   Harvested _____

Planted from   Seeds ☐   Transplant ☐

Plant Type

Fruit ❀	Vegetable ❀	Flower ❀
Herb ❀	Shrub ❀	Tree ❀
Seedling ❀	Annual ❀	Biennial ❀
Perennial ❀	Grass ❀	Weed ❀

Water Requirement   A little 💧   AVG 💧💧   A Lot 💧💧💧

Sunlight Needed   A little ☀   AVG ☀☀   A Lot ☀☀☀

Fertilizers Used _____

Rating   ## Notes

Size   ☆ ☆ ☆ ☆ ☆

Color   ☆ ☆ ☆ ☆ ☆

Taste   ☆ ☆ ☆ ☆ ☆

What's Working?	What's not Working?

Foto

Plant Name _____

Purchased At _____ Price _____

Date Planted _____ Harvested _____

Planted from   Seeds ☐   Transplant ☐

Plant Type

Fruit	Vegetable	Flower
Herb	Shrub	Tree
Seedling	Annual	Biennial
Perennial	Grass	Weed

Water Requirement   A little   AVG   A Lot

Sunlight Needed   A little   AVG   A Lot

Fertilizers Used _____

Rating   Notes

Size   ☆ ☆ ☆ ☆ ☆

Color   ☆ ☆ ☆ ☆ ☆

Taste   ☆ ☆ ☆ ☆ ☆

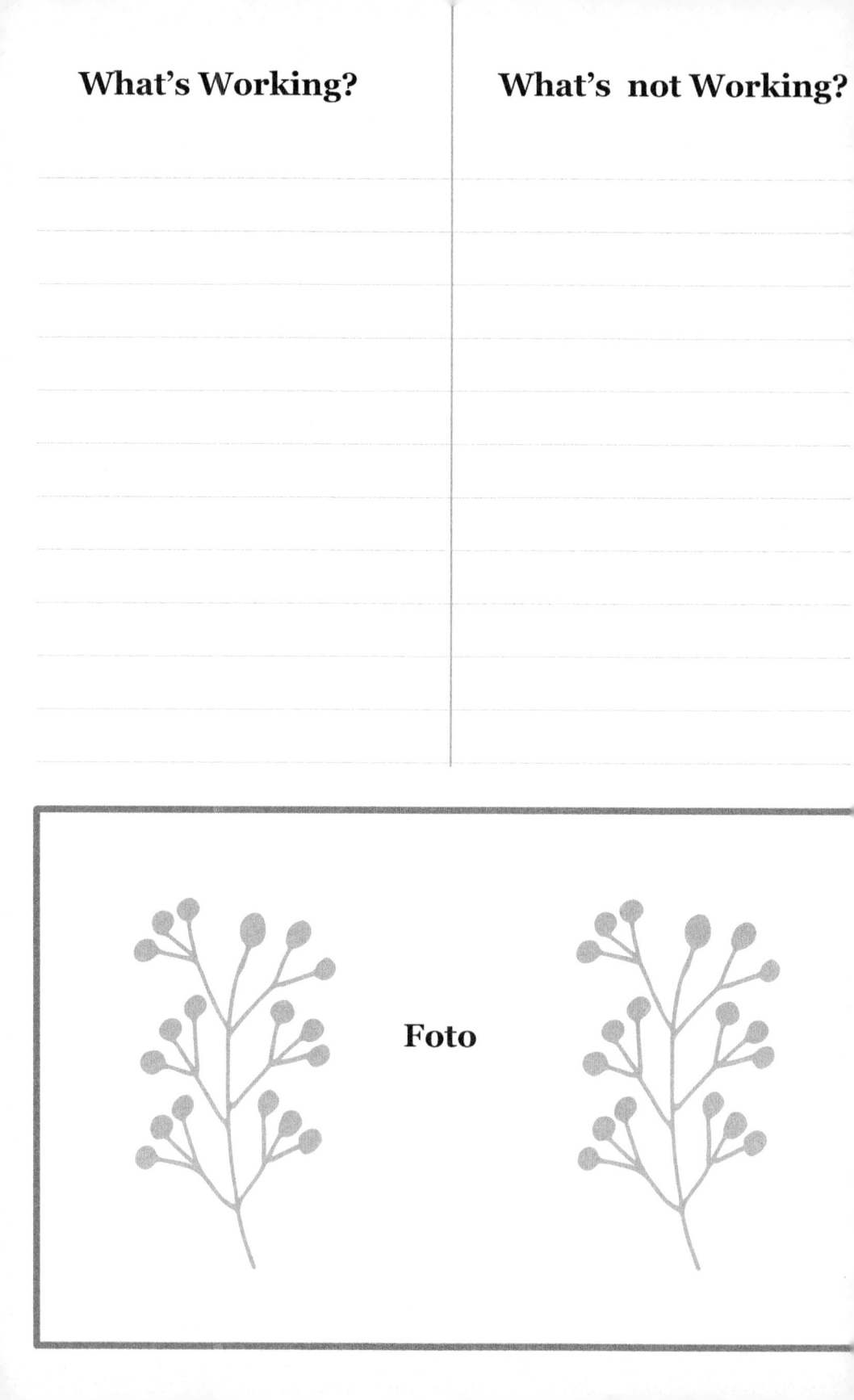

What's Working? | What's not Working?

Foto

Plant Name _____

Purchased At _____ Price _____

Date Planted _____ Harvested _____

Planted from   Seeds ☐   Transplant ☐

Plant Type

Fruit	Vegetable	Flower
Herb	Shrub	Tree
Seedling	Annual	Biennial
Perennial	Grass	Weed

Water Requirement   A little   AVG   A Lot

Sunlight Needed   A little   AVG   A Lot

Fertilizers Used _____

Rating   Notes

Size   ☆ ☆ ☆ ☆ ☆

Color ☆ ☆ ☆ ☆ ☆

Taste ☆ ☆ ☆ ☆ ☆

What's Working?	What's not Working?

Foto

Plant Name _____

Purchased At _____ Price _____

Date Planted _____ Harvested _____

Planted from   Seeds ☐   Transplant ☐

Plant Type

Fruit ✿	Vegetable ✿	Flower ✿
Herb ✿	Shrub ✿	Tree ✿
Seedling ✿	Annual ✿	Biennial ✿
Perennial ✿	Grass ✿	Weed ✿

Water Requirement   A little 💧   AVG 💧💧   A Lot 💧💧💧

Sunlight Needed   A little ☀   AVG ☀☀   A Lot ☀☀☀

Fertilizers Used _____

Rating

Size ☆ ☆ ☆ ☆ ☆

Color ☆ ☆ ☆ ☆ ☆

Taste ☆ ☆ ☆ ☆ ☆

Notes

What's Working? | What's not Working?

Foto

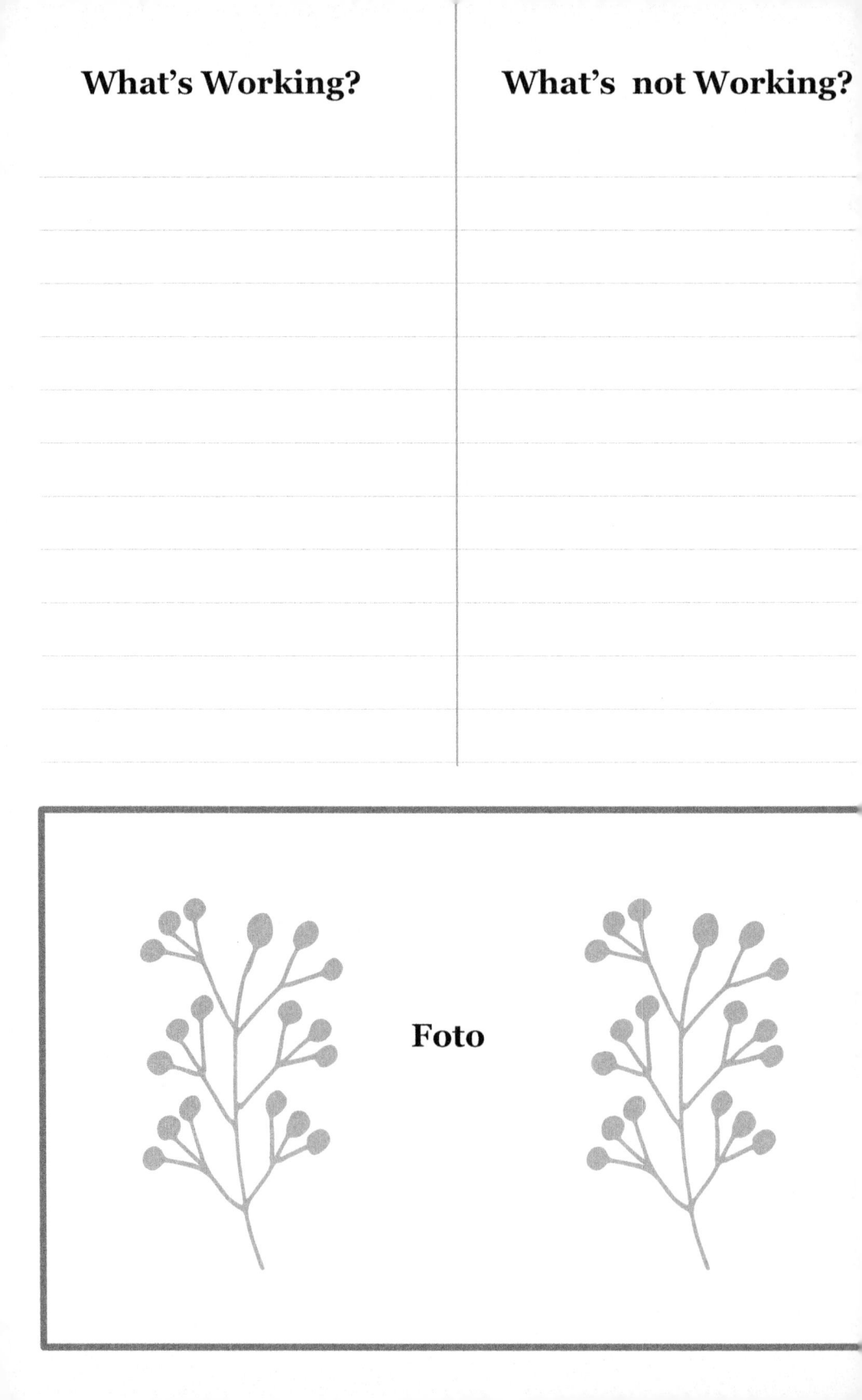

Plant Name _____

Purchased At _____ Price _____

Date Planted _____ Harvested _____

Planted from   Seeds ☐   Transplant ☐

Plant Type

Fruit ✿	Vegetable ✿	Flower ✿
Herb ✿	Shrub ✿	Tree ✿
Seedling ✿	Annual ✿	Biennial ✿
Perennial ✿	Grass ✿	Weed ✿

Water Requirement   A little 💧   AVG 💧💧   A Lot 💧💧💧

Sunlight Needed   A little ☀   AVG ☀☀   A Lot ☀☀☀

Fertilizers Used _____

Rating   ## Notes

Size   ☆ ☆ ☆ ☆ ☆

Color ☆ ☆ ☆ ☆ ☆

Taste ☆ ☆ ☆ ☆ ☆

What's Working?	What's not Working?

Foto

Plant Name _____

Purchased At _____ Price _____

Date Planted _____ Harvested _____

Planted from   Seeds ☐   Transplant ☐

Plant Type

Fruit	Vegetable	Flower
Herb	Shrub	Tree
Seedling	Annual	Biennial
Perennial	Grass	Weed

Water Requirement   A little   AVG   A Lot

Sunlight Needed   A little   AVG   A Lot

Fertilizers Used _____

Rating   ## Notes

Size   ☆ ☆ ☆ ☆ ☆
Color   ☆ ☆ ☆ ☆ ☆
Taste   ☆ ☆ ☆ ☆ ☆

What's Working?	What's not Working?

Foto

Plant Name _____

Purchased At _____ Price _____

Date Planted _____ Harvested _____

Planted from   Seeds ☐   Transplant ☐

Plant Type

Fruit ○	Vegetable ○	Flower ○
Herb ○	Shrub ○	Tree ○
Seedling ○	Annual ○	Biennial ○
Perennial ○	Grass ○	Weed ○

Water Requirement   A little 💧   AVG 💧💧   A Lot 💧💧💧

Sunlight Needed   A little ☀   AVG ☀☀   A Lot ☀☀☀

Fertilizers Used _____

Rating   ## Notes

Size   ☆ ☆ ☆ ☆ ☆

Color   ☆ ☆ ☆ ☆ ☆

Taste   ☆ ☆ ☆ ☆ ☆

What's Working?	What's not Working?

Foto

Plant Name _____

Purchased At _____ Price _____

Date Planted _____ Harvested _____

Planted from   Seeds ☐   Transplant ☐

Plant Type

Fruit ○	Vegetable ○	Flower ○
Herb ○	Shrub ○	Tree ○
Seedling ○	Annual ○	Biennial ○
Perennial ○	Grass ○	Weed ○

Water Requirement   A little 💧   AVG 💧💧   A Lot 💧💧💧

Sunlight Needed   A little ☀   AVG ☀☀   A Lot ☀☀☀

Fertilizers Used _____

Rating   ## Notes

Size   ☆ ☆ ☆ ☆ ☆

Color ☆ ☆ ☆ ☆ ☆

Taste ☆ ☆ ☆ ☆ ☆

What's Working?

What's not Working?

Foto

Plant Name _____

Purchased At _____   Price _____

Date Planted _____   Harvested _____

Planted from   Seeds ☐   Transplant ☐

Plant Type

Fruit ❀	Vegetable ❀	Flower ❀
Herb ❀	Shrub ❀	Tree ❀
Seedling ❀	Annual ❀	Biennial ❀
Perennial ❀	Grass ❀	Weed ❀

Water Requirement   A little 💧   AVG 💧💧   A Lot 💧💧💧

Sunlight Needed   A little ☀   AVG ☀☀   A Lot ☀☀☀

Fertilizers Used _____

Rating   Notes

Size   ☆ ☆ ☆ ☆ ☆
Color ☆ ☆ ☆ ☆ ☆
Taste ☆ ☆ ☆ ☆ ☆

What's Working?	What's not Working?

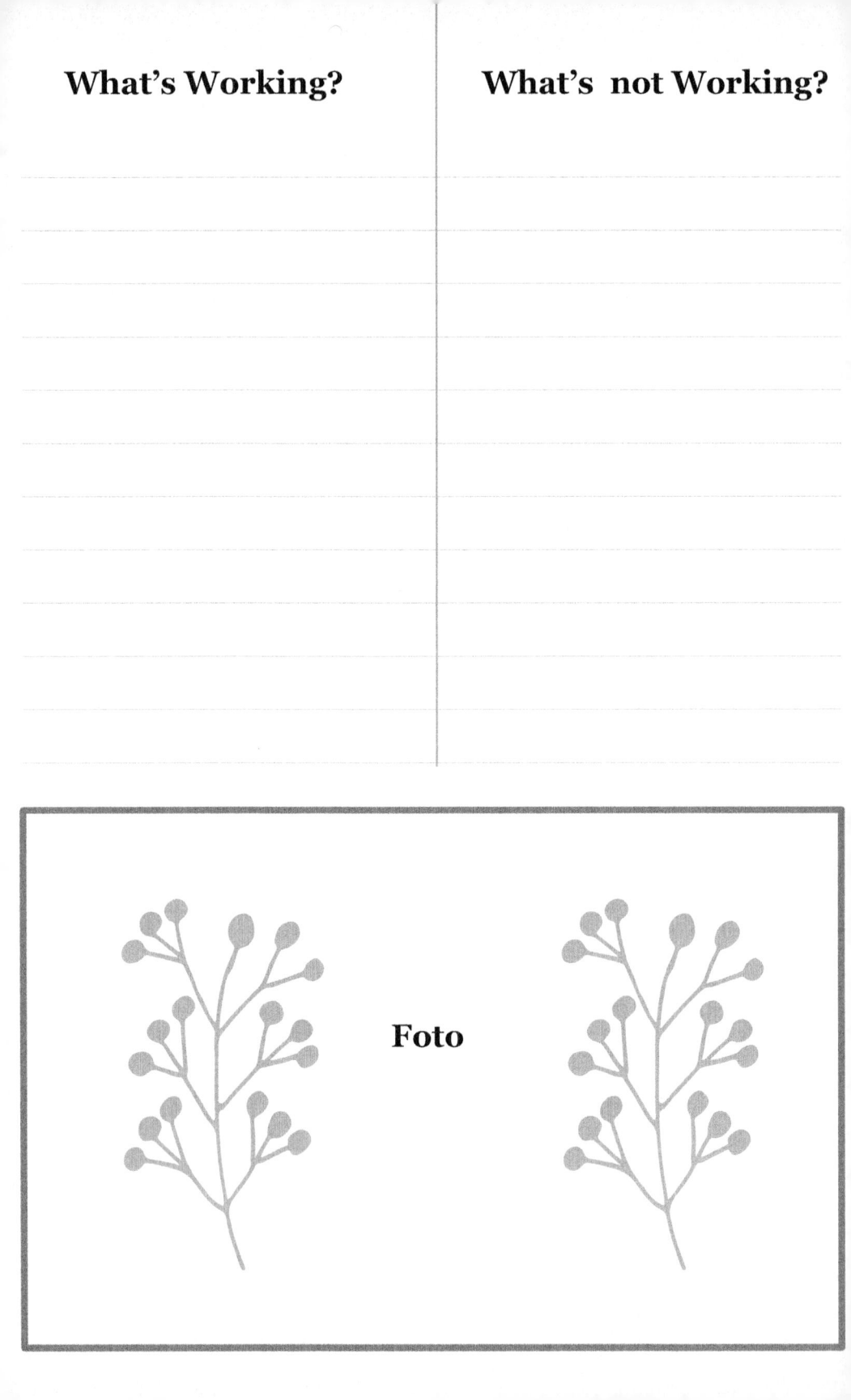

Foto

Plant Name _____

Purchased At _____ Price _____

Date Planted _____ Harvested _____

Planted from   Seeds ☐   Transplant ☐

Plant Type

Fruit ✿	Vegetable ✿	Flower ✿
Herb ✿	Shrub ✿	Tree ✿
Seedling ✿	Annual ✿	Biennial ✿
Perennial ✿	Grass ✿	Weed ✿

Water Requirement   A little 💧   AVG 💧💧   A Lot 💧💧💧

Sunlight Needed   A little ☀   AVG ☀☀   A Lot ☀☀☀

Fertilizers Used _____

Rating   Notes

Size   ☆ ☆ ☆ ☆ ☆

Color   ☆ ☆ ☆ ☆ ☆

Taste   ☆ ☆ ☆ ☆ ☆

What's Working?	What's not Working?

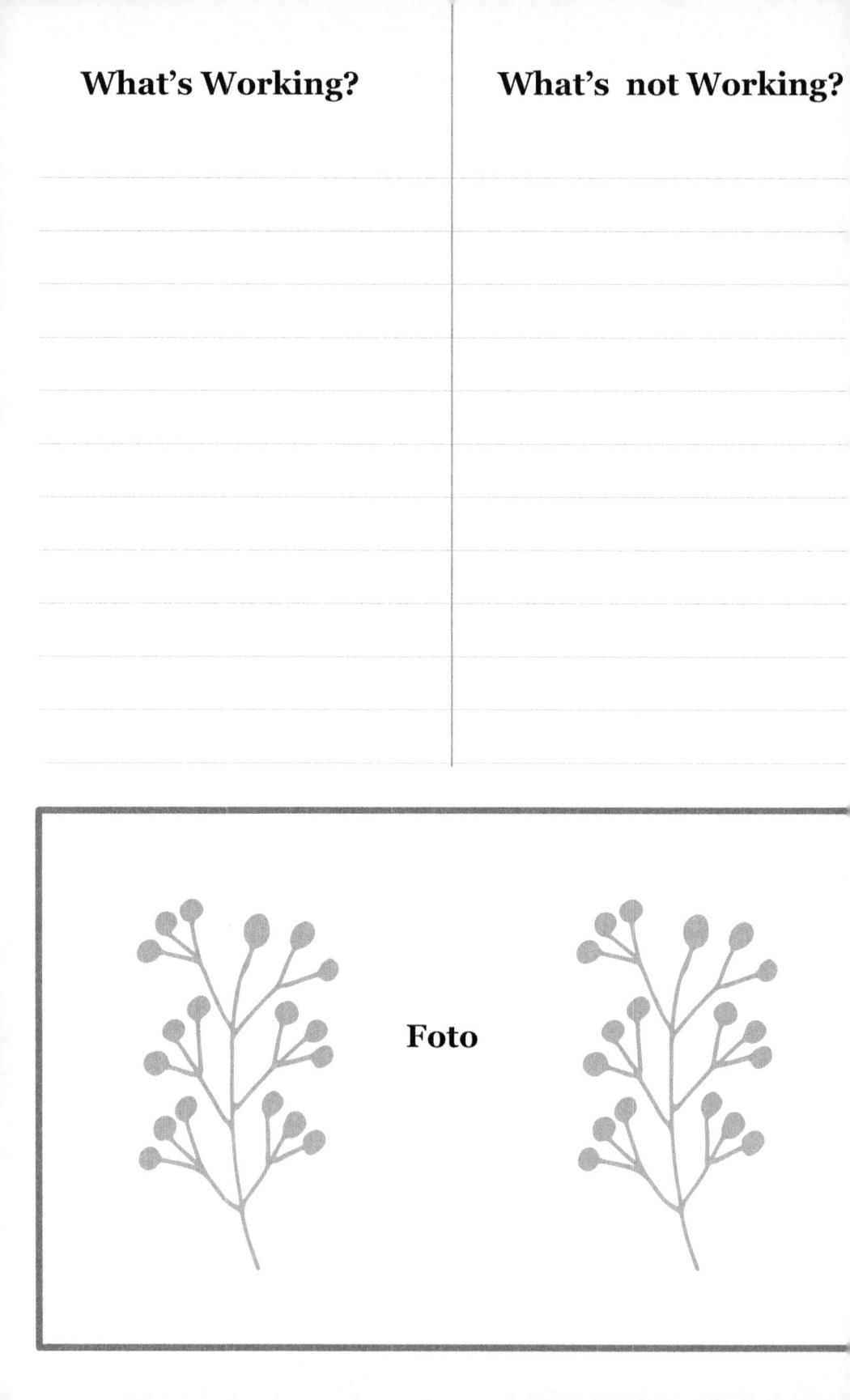

Foto

Notes

Notes

Notes

Notes

Printed in Great Britain
by Amazon